DEVIL ON THE RUN

a DOVE Christian Book by Nicky Cruz

DEVIL on the RUN

by Nicky Cruz

DOVE Christian Books
Melbourne, Florida

DOVE Christian Books, *P.O. Box 36-0122, Melbourne, FL 32936*

*Cover artwork by **Richard Nakamoto***
*Typographical design by **Publications Technologies**, Eau Gallie, Florida*
Printed in the United States of America

CONTENTS

Introduction

Many people today are turning to the glittering attractions of witchcraft, reincarnation, and the dark world of the occult as though it were a brand-new toy. *But I know what it's really like.* I was born and raised in that ugly world.

I know its glittery appeal—*and its cruel realities.*

WHETHER OR NOT YOU READ THIS BOOK, you will see the horrible truth soon, too. A friend in suburban Atlanta recently told how for more than a year, satanism has been a fad at the public school where she teaches. Alarmed, she watched the sudden decline of an 11-year-old honor student. Then she understood: he was hanging around with the older kids in black rock T-shirts who played "devil games" out in the woods.

One day he came to school with rope burns around his neck. He refused to tell school counselors what had happened — and the teacher was heart-broken: by law, she was forbidden to talk about Jesus to him or any other student. Further, school policy obligated her to halt any student trying to share Jesus in class.

But kids dabbling in devil worship were allowed to do so openly. Various teachers were using a variety of occult "novelties" in class since that was what interested the kids. *This was just a phase, she was told by officials.* Last month, the former honor student was found hanging, dead, from a hallway light fixture. In his last seconds of life, he had scratched satanic symbols on the school wall.

Shrugging officials say they are not responsible.

Then who is? You and I, perhaps?

I KNOW I MUST TAKE ACTION. Some time ago, a conviction overwhelmed me. I felt as if God were saying: *Nicky, you know the occult. You've been prepared as no one else to reveal My light in this darkness. You weren't raised to be silent in such a time as this.*

So, I cannot be quiet. The devil is real! Witchcraft and satanism *work* — and bring terrible curses into the lives of all who practice these dark mysteries. I don't want to drag you through the gutter with the excuse that I'm going to "tell all" so that you can see how horrible Lucifer's ancient evil is — *just so I can sell lots of books.*

No, I want you to know how to ***fight back.*** A few years ago, we faced the danger of tremendous increase in exploitation from drugs. That threat will be with us for a long time, but a far greater threat right now is the occult revival.

My biggest fear is that you will glance through this book—maybe just read the "juicy" parts detailing great perverting evil and go on to something else exciting without becoming an effective—*mighty*—spiritual warrior wielding the sword of truth.

My friend, soon ***YOU'RE*** going to have to fight back.

And I want you to **win.**

1

A HORROR-STORY CHILDHOOD

The Caribbean night wind

stirred the jungle outside the famous Spirit House of the feared *jíbaro* Galo Cruz, the "Great One," the rural healer who communed with powerful spirits. The cries of a West Indies woman in labor drifted down through the banana plants, wild bougainvillea, Ixora bushes and the great, rustling laurel and *bucare* trees.

Familiar shrieks of the stubby, nearly extinct Puerto Rico parrot mingled with her cries that evening in our rugged mountains. Echoing in canyons bristling with tree ferns and false-almond trees and coconut palms, the screeches mixed with the raucous night song of the *cokee* tree frog and Caribbean croaking lizards and the calls of the yellow warbler, mockingbird, goldfinch, yellow-shouldered blackbird and pearly-eyed thrasher.

In the moonlight, the thousands of birds and animals — *the boa constrictors, hummingbirds, troupials, woodpeckers and euphonias that make the Sierra de Cayey rain forest a wondrous place for a little boy to play* — did not care that another man-child was coming into their world that night.

AGAIN, MY MOTHER SCREAMED, her weeping blending with the jungle's deafening chorus. Down the hill, desperate visitors waited impatiently for the legendary faith healer to return to his duties, the three-times-a-week *espiritista* — demonic spiritualist — seance where many came and were healed of terrible afflictions.

This evening, they waited, growing amused by ever-louder curses and profanity — obscene Spanish oaths denouncing their much-revered Great One.

"You dog!" screamed a woman's voice they all knew so well — the shrill soprano of Aleja, Galo's wife, the witch who knew the future. "You! Get away from me! You're the one who did this to me — *AGAIN!* Ahhhhhhhh! No! *Uhhhhhhhhh!*" A new labor contraction convulsed the mother-to-be.

Patiently, Galo, who was also called *El Curandero,* the Healer, clutched her hand. But he was in a trance, making magic with the great spirits. His lips moved silently in foreign languages his mind did not recognize as he interceded for his beautiful wife. In another mystical world so very far away — yet all around them — he was battling demons and throwing back evil forces ... and was only dimly unaware of her loud accusations.

His forehead furrowed, his brow beaded with sweat, he muttered great, powerful spells to ward away bad spirits. Urgently he pleaded for help from the "good" phantasms he knew so well.

LIKE ANY DEVOTED FATHER, he had hopes and dreams for this child — who would be his eighth son. This one would be *strong.* He would follow in the footsteps of his father's father, grandfather and great-grandfather to make magnificent magic, bind away evil and heal the sick.

As Aleja screamed and cursed him, Galo was waging battle in the way that he knew best — in the spirit world. He mumbled incantations that made great evil gods of the earth tremble before him. Unafraid, he invoked the aid of his many lifelong spirit allies — whom he believed to be the good souls of mighty saints of God — to help him defeat the evil titans and bring health and blessing to this new child.

Amid it all, an attending midwife calmly did her job, urging Aleja to push the little boy into the world of the living.

Aleja screamed and cursed. Galo calmly did battle in the heavenlies. And the sick gathering at the Spirit House waited. You see, in the mountains of our bullet-shaped Caribbean island, so gently cooled by trade winds, Jesus Christ was just a name.

Most of the poor banana farmers and poorer sugar cane workers and destitute coffee-bean pickers put their faith in their ancestors' old spirit gods. They sought favor from the good and evil demons of the long-vanquished *Carib* and *Taino* Indians, who called their emerald island

Borinquen. They searched for peace through the ancient demonic traditions of African slaves brought to work the plantations in the early years.

THESE GOOD, FEAR-FILLED PEOPLE believed in God, too — for theirs was a rich Spanish heritage. Their forefathers were the explorers seeking a western route to India, Cathay and Arabia. Christopher Columbus. Ponce de Leon. Hernando Cortez and all the terrible *conquistadores* that forced Christianity into the New World at sword-point.

If you had asked the trembling, yearning visitors to the Spirit House, many would have claimed to be good Christians. Yet, over the years, the true faith brought by missionaries to the Greater Antilles Islands had become twisted and unholy — filled with terror and superstition easily manipulated by powerful spirit-healers such as *El Taumaturgo*, Galo Cruz, the Miracle Worker.

A baby's cry broke the stillness.

THE MIDWIFE LIFTED THE NEW ARRIVAL by his ankles and gave him a gentle swat on the buttocks. She smiled as he let out a healthy howl. "A boy," she announced, placing the baby into Aleja's anxious arms.

But Galo had already known days before. The spirits had told him it would be a son. And this one would be different.

Galo had decided to name the new arrival after the great saint San Nicolas — the old spirit that American children today call Santa Claus.

"Yes," had said Galo, watching the midwife cut the umbilical cord. "This one will be called Nicky."

San Nicolas de la Cruz. Saint Nicholas of the Holy Cross.
Nicky Cruz.

AND THEN MY FATHER RETURNED to his patients. Just days before, a man had been brought in a hammock to our compound at Las Piedras, a peasant village in the shadow of *El Yunque* mountain in the Caribbean National Forest. His leg was so swollen it was feared he would die.

"Bring me healing leaves," my father had said to Mama. Although the hour that she would give birth to me was approaching, she had hobbled out to the garden and returned with a great basket of dark, green leaves. These Papa spread liberally over the discolored, swollen leg.

Papa cupped a pitcher of water between his big hands and spoke loudly — with great authority. *"San Miguel, San Espedisto, spirits of strength and life,"* he prayed loudly as he seemed to look into unfathomable distances, *"bind the spirit of evil that attacked my brother. As water cools fire, set apart this water to cool my brother's fever and drive out his sickness."*

Papa had sprinkled the water over the leaf-covered leg. The man had groaned and his friends dropped to their knees, moaning and praying.

"When you drink this water," declared Papa, "you will be healed."

He lifted the man's head with one hand and held the vessel to his lips with the other. "Drink!" he commanded. "Drink all of it!"

Weakly, the man obeyed. As onlookers stared in horror, suddenly the miraculous occured. Five long *things* that looked like worms slithered out of his toe. My father sat back, exhausted.

The swelling immediately began to go down.

BUT SUCH HEALINGS were everyday occurrences in our compound. The Spirit House was a small building with a circular table inside where Mama, Papa, and others gathered for their sessions with spirits. Sometimes they met there all day, sometimes in the evenings for several hours, calling on the "good" spirits for help.

You see, although my parents were using the terrible power of Satan and his demons, they were deceived into believing that there are good demonic spirits and bad demonic spirits.

Of course, my Mama and Papa claimed that they only sought the aid of good spirits. But, I know now that they kept a terrible secret. They denied it even to themselves.

But they knew. We were in the devil's grip.

BUT, JESUS CHRIST LOVED THAT LITTLE BABY nursing at the breast of the feared witch of Las Piedras — little Nicky, eighth son of *El Taumaturgo*, the Charmer.

I got terribly sick two months after I was born when, I believe, the devil saw something in me that gave him immense fear. He acted right away to kill me. He just about succeeded.

I almost died.

I was consumed to the bones. I could not hold anything in my stomach. My father was powerless to break the illness. My mother chanted spells and implored the demon spirits. But they would do nothing. I was dying.

My father went crazy with grief. But my mother was filled with anger. I was evil, she said. "He came to curse us!" she screamed at Papa. "He is the son of Satan!"

"No," said my father calmly. "I want my son to live." He went outside and came back in with a black hen — one of my mother's favorite chickens and a good egg-layer, too. As she protested, he began one of his most powerful and ancient rituals, chanting and casting a mighty spell. Suddenly, he chopped off the hen's head and let its blood pour all over my little two-month-old body.

THEN HE BEGAN TO GO INTO A DEEP TRANCE, praying aloud in a horrible, ugly language that wasn't at all from heaven.

And I got well. *Yes!*

Do not doubt the power of evil forces. Frankly, I am convinced that they *constantly war with each other* as well as against the forces of good.

Ah, you may be asking: *Did the demons make you well, Nicky?* Well, I don't like the idea either. But I saw my father make lots of people completely whole again.

And yes, I also believe that Jesus Christ had His hand on me from the day that I was born — and that He had a plan for my life.

He would not let the devil take my life.

BUT MY MOTHER'S GRUDGE AGAINST ME grew strong. She hated her eighth son. Although I didn't realize it as a little boy, I was severely abused — physically, emotionally and verbally. I was the one who got whipped and screamed at when she was angry at all the other kids. *I took the blame*.

I, too, grew resentful and angry. And sneaky. And mean. At school, I was constantly in serious trouble. The teachers were scared of me — and even more frightened of my legendary parents.

But I never understood why school officials were always kind to my brothers and to my little sister — but so harsh with me.

I did not realize.

I had the curse of my forefathers.

The evil that my father practiced was destined for me. I would be the Great One to follow him.

WHEN I WAS EIGHT YEARS OLD, my mother and I had a terrible confrontation that changed my life.

"I hate you, " she screamed one day — in unexpected fury. "I don't love you. You have been cursed from the day you were born! I hate you! You aren't my son. You are the son of Satan! Get out of this house! I don't want to see you!"

I was destroyed. I stood there devastated.

"No, Mama," I pleaded, trembling, "that's not true! I love you!"

"Well, I don't love you!" she shrieked, grabbing me and shaking me. Her long, sharp fingernails cut my skin. "You are a curse on us! I hate you."

I believe that she was scared of me. Or even worse, the great evil demonic forces that possessed her feared me as a rival and a threat!

"Mama!" I cried, "you're hurting me!"

She and several other mediums had been sitting around the house drinking coffee. Now, in front of them, she denounced her little boy in a demonic sing-song. "No, you're not mine, not mine ... hand of Lucifer upon his life ... finger of Satan touch his life ... finger of Satan touch his soul ... mark of the beast on his heart ... no, not my son, not mine!"

VARIOUS DEMONS BEGAN TO SPEAK through her, some with the voice of a man, some with the voice of women. "You are the son of Satan!" they howled, mocking me. "Get out. Go out of this house! You are not welcome here."

Although I was just a little boy, I knew my mother was controlled by things incredibly strong and hideous. I knew it wasn't really my Mama speaking to me like that. Not *really*. My Mama loved me — even though she cursed me in the night and spat her hatred at me all day long.

"I love you, Mama," I wept.

"Well, I hate you," she sneered. "You are not any son of mine. You are the devil's son, sent here to destroy us. I hate you, I hate you, I hate you."

FROM THAT DAY, I WAS ON MY OWN — emotionally at least. I wept and hid in the dust under our house, covering myself with dirt. That evening my father sought me out, roughly calling me a little piglet.

But I was no longer an innocent little boy. I ran away and hid in the forest for several nights with my only true friends — the parrots and the fireflies and the singing tree frogs.

I swam in the cool brooks and watched the big fish. I tried to catch minnows. And emotionally, I shriveled up until I was unable to care about anybody or anything except my own survival.

I did not ever cry again during my childhood. My tears dried up. My heart hardened to stone.

Defiantly, I came home several mornings later and was allowed to stay. My father wouldn't let her physically kick me out at age eight. He even tried to spend a little time with me — and called me by my pet-name: *Little Bird*.

BUT I KNEW THAT I WAS ALONE. He was too busy with his horrible profession. And I was just one of 18 children. There was no time for me.

My mother and I became increasingly spiteful enemies — an absolutely hellish relationship for any little boy. *I needed her love.* She was my Mama. I desperately loved her — although I swore that I hated her and would someday kill her.

She would be strangely affectionate to me at times — but unpredictably vicious the next moment. Deep in her trances, she would hold me on her lap, then unexpectedly shriek new threats and denunciations while my father sat ashen-faced and silent. I learned not to let down my guard — not to let her touch me ... yet the little boy within me hungered, ached for my Mama's approval and caresses.

I believe the demonic forces that filled my mother delighted in my ever-increasing confusion and anger — and took every opportunity to torment me and send me into defeat, depression and wild, vengeful troublemaking. I began to believe without a doubt that I was nobody. Not even my mother could love me. By age nine, I began to stay away for days, then weeks on end — haunting the streets of the nearby town of Humacao, sleeping in alleys, playing on the windswept beach and stealing to eat.

Although I was just a child, I knew I could trust no one. I could love no one. It was *me* against the world.

And I was going to win. And all around me, the unseen demons laughed. Satan smiled. He had big plans for me.

I was truly his son.

You may be stunned

by some new, horrible TV special on devil worship. Safe in your home, you may shiver as you read some lurid article in the supermarket tabloids of satanists sacrificing infants in honor of Satan.

But from the experiences during the 15 years that I lived in and around my parents' demon-worship compound at Las Piedras, I can testify to you that whatever horrified you was just the tip of the iceberg.

You haven't seen anything. *I grew up in it.* I survived nightmarish evil. I lived through its hideousness. I know its reality like only a child robbed of his innocence can know.

Friend, today human sacrifice is real in our "modern" world. Worship of the dark and terrible is sweeping our "civilized" world, spread through such clever media as rock music, bestselling books and TV. Children are disappearing at a shocking rate from our streets as worshipers of this evil feed the hunger of their dark lord for the blood of innocents.

You scoff? It has happened before — just read your Bible's accounts of human sacrifice and the terrible curses that the Israelites brought on their nation as they laid their infants on demonic altars. Then, read history.

And praise Almighty God that you — living in God's love — have not known the ugliness and terror Satan serves to those he believes are his.

I've just watched a sickening video of a TV journalist interviewing avowed American and Canadian satanists — including murderers, some serving life sentences without parole, some awaiting execution.

ON DEATH ROW, A SNEERING KILLER BRAGS that he will reign over 10,000 souls in hell for all eternity in return for giving Satan a nice, brutal murder.

In a rally, a crowd shrieks its hideous approval as a satanic leader rants on and on about their demonic *right* as predators to kill and terrorize the weak and defenseless. He spits his hatred of Christians.

In a TV studio, a trembling woman tells in hushed tones of how as a satanic cult member she was forced to give up her two small children to be used as human sacrifices. Their hearts were ripped out and offered to Satan. Their flesh and blood was used in the satanic communion service. Her voice cracks, her hand trembles. There is a ghoulish ring of truth to her testimony.

You may tremble in terror. *Don't.*

Friend, I'm neither shocked nor threatened. No evil that any of these poor, deluded people might like to perpetrate on you, me or any other obedient, Christian believer can prosper.

We are victorious. *I didn't always know that.*

I hesitate to write on this topic.

Always before I have stopped short. Frankly, people look at me in disbelief when I try to describe my childhood.

Furthermore, I despise Christian books that are full of nothing but "horror stories for believers." Too many followers of Jesus get caught up in the shocking ugliness of this or that supposed conspiracy — *which may or may not really be out to get us.*

When I speak in person, I can feel the crowd stirring with interest when I talk about the devil and about witches who confront me in airports or in revivals. They like to hear about my horrifying childhood, raised in the middle of spirit worship in rural Puerto Rico.

But if I am not careful, I do terrible damage to the cause of Christ as

I talk about the witches and satanists and New Agers who hate us so terribly. If I do not follow the leading of the Holy Spirit and give hope and victory to these fine Christians, they will not leave my meeting filled with a yearning to win the lost to Jesus.

Instead, they will go home and have nightmares.

They will worry about demons lying in wait to get them.

THEY WILL TURN ON THE TV AND BE HORRIFIED as some secular journalist plays a rerun of an old Charles Manson interview once again — and as the avowed devil-worshiper and unashamed murderer rants on and on about what horrible vengeance he will bring upon the earth if he can only "get up to that highway" — escape from prison.

Their hearts pound as they read newspaper accounts of the latest satanic murders committed by teen-age devil worshipers. Of the four buddies who at age 17 got deeper and deeper into drugs, heavy metal rock music and, then, ritual mutilation of animals, drinking the poor creatures' blood. Of how it was not violent enough. Of how three of the four turned on the other and, laughing, bashed his head in with the baseball bats they'd just used to destroy a cat. "Why me, why me?" pleaded their friend as he gasped his last breaths. Their answer: "Because it's fun, Steve!"

Terrified Christians hearing of these things lose sight of an important truth: *God created all things.*

He alone is God.

Our Almighty Father is the one who created a beautiful archangel called Lucifer who once upon a time was one of the most powerful beings in heaven. But Lucifer chose to challenge God and was cast from heaven — with the angels who rebelled with him.

Sure, today he stalks the earth like a hungry coyote.

He *knows* he blew it.

He knows that his time is growing short.

IT IS HARD FOR GOOD CHRISTIANS to understand his great darkness or his hunger to destroy anything the Creator has made. Cast from heaven, doomed to eternal agony, today he is hideously spiteful, bitter, vengeful.

He is *so* jealous of humans. *Why?* We alone are created in God's own image. We alone are so greatly loved by the Creator! We are destined to enjoy eternity in His presence ... while Lucifer will be spending the trillions of years to come in agony and punishment and darkness and loneliness.

Lucifer knows that soon he will be humiliated one last time before all creation — destroyed, never again to bask in the marvelous presence of the One Who Created All.

Instead, humans will enjoy that privilege forever and ever. Lucifer will be forever banished, defeated, shamed and repudiated. A failure.

Lucifer cannot turn from his ways.

God will *not* forgive him, the archangel who took an eternally damning ego trip — and challenged the Master of the Universe.

So, my friend,

just who should we fear? This defeated, vengeful angel thrown out of heaven? Our Almighty protector, the Lord God, is our *loving Father*. He delights in our obedience. He enjoys our praises. We are the apple of his eye.

Furthermore, He is the *only God*. That infuriates Lucifer. He knows that whatever he pretends to do is only a dim imitation of true creation. God reigns supreme. No power can challenge Him and prevail. He made all things. He can wave His mighty hand and cause anything that displeases Him to pass away. *All creation exists at his pleasure.*

I am trying to get you to understand a simple phrase that you've probably sung or read or heard hundreds of times:

He alone is God.

Don't you see the power in that?

Our great and loving Father, alone, is God.

SO SHOULD WE SHRINK IN TERROR at the awful things that Lucifer and his followers might do to us? Should we tremble in the night, frightened that some hellish cultist may snatch our babies, molest our children, burn our homes or put some nasty curse on our prosperity?

No! Our God watches over the obedient believer!

Walk with me on the dark side, my Christian friend, for a while. Let us understand a bit about the evil that hates us so.

But let us not fear.

For our mighty, loving, protecting Father, *alone,* is God.

2

GROWING UP
WITH *ESPIRITISTAS*

As a little boy, I snickered

as I spied on people trudging hesitantly up to our property, fearfully glancing around — worried that some kind of evil was going to jump out of the shadows and devour their souls.

Often I was tempted to leap out of my hiding place and yell "Boo!" But I knew better. These trusting, nervous people were my family's livelihood.

Sometimes I was playing under the house when Mama answered their knock at the door. I listened as they stammered out their requests for her to tell their fortunes or heal their ailments — or summon loved ones from beyond the grave.

"Contacting the dead" was Mama's specialty. In psychic terms, she was believed to be very "sensitive" and served as a gateway for spirits to speak to the living. In our living room, Mama and Papa and our paying customers would sit in a circle and wait for a ghost to reveal its presence.

You are probably wondering if I believe Mama really contacted the dead. During my boyhood, everyone I knew took it for granted.

I REMEMBER ONE NIGHT WHEN MY GRANDFATHER was supposedly summoned from beyond the grave. He described in rich detail things he and I had done together when I was very little and we were very close. Then, he gave me a real tongue-lashing — telling me to straighten up and quit being a troublemaker.

Everyone believed that Mama and Papa not only talked to the dead, but did their healing work with the help of the deceased — particularly the most holy saints of the Bible.

Today, I know that God's Word says we live once and then are judged by Him before going on to our reward or eternal punishment — and that there is no return from either place. So, what supernatural force convincingly pretended to be my grandfather that night? *A demon.* One of Satan's evil co-workers.

I believe our beautiful jungle property was crawling with such diabolic presences. Whenever she went into a trance, Mama allowed these evil, lying spirits to take hold of her and speak through her — demons with the ability to pretend to be loved ones sending messages from beyond the grave.

Why would Satan and his angels pay any attention to a little rural compound in Puerto Rico? Because humans there were willing to do his dirty work. Oh, what great public relations my parents did: advising about future events, healing the sick, "contacting" the dear departed. And as they did it, they demonstrated that God is not nearly as powerful as the spirit world.

And that is such a terrible lie!

OUR MIGHTY FATHER SO LOVES PUERTO RICO, emerald isle of my youth, one of the Caribbean Sea's Greater Antilles Islands. Puerto Rico is a tropical paradise of 3.4 million or so United States citizens. That's right! We're Americans! When the U.S. won the Spanish-American War in 1898, it took possession of the Virgin Islands, Puerto Rico and Cuba.

Cuba was given its independence — which I'm sure the politicians regret now. But America hung onto beautiful Puerto Rico. *Smart move!* We are the fourth biggest island in the Caribbean Sea — only nearby Cuba, Hispaniola and Jamaica are larger. Someday, I believe in my heart, we will become a state, just like Hawaii out in the South Pacific finally did.

Like Hawaii, it's always cool in Puerto Rico — the average temperature is in the upper 70s. Like Hawaii, most of our island is made up of rugged mountains covered with lush rain forests. And also like Hawaii, we have a beautiful, sapphire sea gently lapping our gorgeous sun-drenched beaches. Breath-taking reefs attract thousands of vacationing snorklers and scuba divers.

BUT WE HAVE SOMETHING TERRIBLE in common with Hawaii. You may not know that Hawaii has a serious problem of *kapu,* native demon-worship. All around the islands, one can find shrines to good and evil spirits. On Oahu, if you visit the ruins of ancient Puu O Mahuka Heiau or other old cities of refuge, you'll notice that everywhere are little stacks of rocks. In between each layer, you'll see a fresh banana leaf.

These are offerings to the old Hawaiian gods.

Once you recognize what they are, you'll see these little offerings are everywhere. On the Big Island of Hawaii, great power is believed to be held by Pele, the red-haired goddess of the volcano. Locals often refuse to joke about her — for fear that the ground will open up and molten lava will destroy their property ... something that actually occurs on the Big Island, with or without offending Pele.

Witchcraft is strong in Hawaii, too.

SOME OF THE MOST POWERFUL PEOPLE in Hawaii are *kahunas,* witchdoctors. Some years ago, the *kahunas* took offense when the World Football League decided to put its Hawaiian franchise in a new stadium on the site of an old Hawaiian *heiau* or shrine.

The *kahunas* warned the owners to find another site.

Laughing, the mainlanders took their warning as a joke. Sure, find another spot or the devil's gonna get us. You bet!

So, the *kahunas* put a curse on the stadium and on the owners and the World Football League. Well, every terrible thing that you can imagine happened at the construction site. Workmen died. Accidents cost the owners hundreds of thousands of dollars. The season started and the team had nowhere to play.

Work constantly ground to a standstill.

Finally, the team folded.

Then, the World Football League itself went bankrupt. Happily, the *kahunas* took total credit.

WELL, IF YOU VISIT MY BEAUTIFUL PUERTO RICO, you'll find that we have the same sort of thing. *Espiritistas* are everywhere. They are widely respected.

Witches.

Just like my mom and dad. That's what they liked to be called: *espiritistas.* Witches, witchdoctors, satanic high priests, psychics, sorcerers, mediums and spiritualists are terms I sometimes use in the pulpit to try to explain just exactly what my mom and dad were.

Here's what *National Geographic* magazine said about *espiritistas* in an April 1983 article called *The Uncertain State of Puerto Rico*. Author Bill Richards wrote:

"... I felt less at ease when Felipe led me to a wooden shack whose walls were papered down to the last inch with pictures of saints. A round Buddha meditated on a shelf.

"Casimira, an espiritista *in a flowered dress, works here. Business-men, lawyers, even doctors, it is said, have been coming to her with their cares and their pains for more than half a century. In predominantly Roman Catholic Puerto Rico,* espiritistas *are a well-accepted second line of defense.*

" 'I get my power from the saints,' the 70-year-old spiritualist told me. "But it is hard work taking care of all these things. I tried to stop years ago because I was tired. But so many people needed help I couldn't quit."

"At my request Casimira obligingly read my future. She shuffled a deck of worn cards and began laying them out on a table. My birth date? A few more cards were slapped down. She reached into a glass bowl filled with water and sprinkled a little on me. Then she looked up and smiled.

"The rest of my stay in Puerto Rico was sure to be filled with good luck, she said — buy a few lottery tickets, who knows? I would find great beauty ... a blonde with green eyes ..."

Well, it sounds as if *National Geographic* went to visit Mama.

BEGINNING IN HER TEENS IN THE LATE 1920s, she was active in spiritualistic meetings in San Juan, the capitol of our Caribbean island. She seemed to have a natural gift for psychic things.

When handsome, rugged faith healer Galo Cruz came from the mountains to the big city, he was immediately drawn to the beautiful *espiritista*. And she was very taken with him, too. Soon after their wedding they moved to the country and set up the spiritualist compound in Las Piedras.

MY DAD WAS BIG AND STRONG in both physique and spirit. He was the kind of person who didn't need to raise his voice to command respect. He fairly radiated quiet power. As our family grew, my brothers and I were scared to death when we thought he might find out about something bad we had done, for he was a strict disciplinarian.

Yet he was kind as well as firm. We knew that he loved us, and we adored him. Other people did, too, by the hundreds. Papa had an outgoing personality and a great sense of humor. You can get an idea of what people thought of my father from the fact 20 years after he died, people still came to our property in Las Piedras looking for him to help them.

WHEN PAPA NOTICED SOMEONE ELSE with occult powers, he often brought him to our compound for training. One of these trainees, a man named Gomez, once began acting as if he were in charge when Papa was away on a trip.

When my father returned, he heard of what had gone on and took Gomez into the Spirit House. As Papa talked, Gomez began to look cold and white and as frightened as anyone I've ever seen.

"To do a thing of this kind," Papa said, "it is not enough to have the gifts and the mystic talents. These you have. But unless you learn how to use them properly, you may arouse such powers of destruction as you cannot imagine!"

It was a typically sunny Puerto Rican day, but Papa had barely uttered these words when the sky suddenly became very dark. A flash of lightning shot across the sky and an enormous clap of thunder exploded so loudly that the very ground seemed to shake. Gomez fell sobbing to the ground, begging forgiveness.

PAPA AND MAMA SAID THEY BELIEVED good spirits gave our family protection — but said they both had to be on guard against evil spirits. They believed that when they summoned the help of the good spirits, evil spirits often came with them.

So they took every precaution to keep the evil ones away.

Today I believe *all* their spirit helpers were evil.

Some may have had grudges against each other — for it seemed that they often battled each other. But all were demonic.

Evil.

They were not co-workers with Almighty God.

THEIR EVIL AFFECTED US in many, many ways. Although on the surface it appeared that we were normal and loving, we were a bitterly unhappy family, .

Even so, Mama was a marvelous co-worker with Papa. She often permitted the afflictions of those who came to us for help to enter her own body, so that she and Papa might learn the cause and seek the cure.

One evening, for example, when I was a little boy, a young woman pulled up her skirts and made remarks that made Mama look grim and Papa look embarrassed. Then, suddenly, the girl's face looked like an old man's and she began to speak in an elderly, slow, trembling voice. Suddenly Mama began acting — even looking — exactly like the girl. The young lady slumped down onto the cot as a trickle of white froth ran from a corner of Mama's mouth.

Papa ordered everyone to concentrate as he sat intensely still, his big hand over Mama's. For a long time he sat like a statue, gazing at Mama as though he could not tear his eyes away. Finally he relaxed and spoke.

"Aleja," he said, "has taken this girl's malady upon herself so that she could help me cure her. Now I know what to do."

Papa looked around the building. His gaze came to rest on a lizard clinging to the wall near a window.

Papa said, "This girl's malady must enter into that lizard. When it does she will be cured."

ALL OF A SUDDEN THE LIZARD LEAPED out the window like a shot. The girl sat up on her cot. Mama straightened up as though she had just awakened from a long sleep.

My father and mother often cooperated in this way to accomplish amazing results. Mama was able to enter into such complete empathy with an afflicted person that she bore that person's sickness or trouble in her own mind and body. When this transfer had been made, Mama opened her mind to the spirits, who told her the real cause of the affliction.

Then, often without words, Papa communicated with Mama to learn the cause and remove it. But all this ordinarily happened while Mama was in a state of deep trance, and afterward she usually had no memory of what had happened.

It was not pleasant or easy, to bear the sufferings of all who came to the center. It wasn't always certain what might happen.

Once when Papa and Mama were treating a patient in the Spirit House, a demon came upon Mama with such force that she was catapulted clear over the table.

Sometimes she was possessed with such a furious presence that it took many men and women to hold her. And my mother was never a large or muscular person.

But their reputation

was so great that often there were sick people in hammocks and on stretchers and cots all around our little stucco residence next to the Spirit House.

Others were brought in for the services on Mondays, Wednesdays and Fridays at the Spirit House.

During those services, there was usually a crystal ball or a glass of water in the center of the table. Everyone at the table concentrated on this while the good spirits were invoked. Mama sat next to him until Papa gave her permission to "let go."

Papa would not do this until he was sure no evil spirits were present. The ring of hands was believed to keep them out.

Then Mama would go into a trance.

It was occasionally a horrible thing to see.

She was never a kind, gentle person when I was a little boy. Small children were always terrified of her.

But when she went into a trance, she could become a horrible, evil entity straight from the pits of hell. Other times, she would simply begin to give personal advice to those in the room or greetings from "the other side" — dead friends and relatives.

YOU MAY BE SURPRISED that we kids were allowed to participate. Actually, we weren't. Only very rarely were we allowed in since we didn't take the whole thing very seriously. On the rare occasions that we were allowed in, we were usually thrown out since we'd giggle or whisper and break the mood.

Most of the time, we would peek in the window.

But more often than not, we just skipped out since we considered the whole business boring.

I hope that gives hope to parents who are distressed because their eight-year-olds yawn and complain at church even when the Holy Spirit is moving in a mighty way. Impressive, evil magic was happening right in front of our eyes, yet we kids were bored to tears.

In fact, I grew to resent my parents' profession. I blamed it for the way that the teachers treated me at school — like some sort of dangerous criminal. I hated how my buddies' parents seemed to be frightened of me and my brothers.

And I hated how the kids mocked me on the playground.

"His mama's a *bruja!* His mama's a *bruja!*" they would sneer in the cruel sing-song way that kids do to one another.

And I was defenseless, since it was pointless to deny what everybody knew. My mother *was* a *bruja* — a witch.

ONCE WHEN MY PARENTS WERE HOLDING a seance in our home with some other mediums, my six-year-old brother Rafi came into the room and sidled up to Mama. Suddenly she shot out her hands and held him so tightly around the neck that he began to scream, "Mama, what's wrong with you?"

Mama remembers it this way:

"I couldn't understand what Rafi was saying. Another identity had taken complete control of my mind and body. My husband looked at me and ordered the spirit to leave me. When it left, I felt weak and exhausted; I could not remember anything that had happened."

Of course this murderous impulse was completely uncharacteristic of Mama, for both she and Papa deeply loved little Rafi.

THEY LOVED MY LITTLE SISTER, TOO. Her story is a terrible tragedy that I cannot tell in complete detail yet — for Carmen has taken on the task of continuing Mama and Papa's *espiritista* work. I was only 7 years old, but I remember when it started with her: during one seance, the 4-year-old was gripped in the clutches of something truly horrible.

It held little Carmen unconscious for long hours as my father tried to work his magic over her to deliver her. When she came back to her senses, she was different, though. She did not utter a word for more than two weeks. For a long time, half of her face was paralyzed.

Although she recovered physically, she was never the same innocent baby again.

Today, she sneers at the message of Jesus Christ and professes to be a dedicated *espiritista*. I love my sister very much and would not do anything to humiliate her, so let me say that I pray constantly for her — and would appreciate your doing the same. Our Almighty Father loves her greatly.

Someday, I believe, my beautiful little sister will be a great co-worker in God's family. But today ... I can only wait and pray.

SOMETIMES MAMA WOULD SPREAD OUT a pack of tarot cards while she looked at one of us children, and we knew she was looking at our future lives.

But she didn't need tarot cards to tell many things about a person. After one woman in Las Piedras dropped in for a visit, Mama said matter-of-factly, "She will die soon." The next day the woman was struck by a careening car that ran up onto the sidewalk where she was standing, and died on the way to the hospital. But the cards gave Mama a complete picture of a person's future. However, she never talked to any of us eighteen children about what she had learned. She must have realized that some things are best left alone.

Soon after Mama and Papa moved to Las Piedras, Mama saw the Great Depression coming. She had a vision of many acres of ground burned over, and she saw the economic destruction coming. Mama advised the people who came to our house to start saving for hard times, and in the bleak days of the 1930s many of them remembered her warnings.

ON JANUARY 6, 1940, A SPIRIT VISITED MAMA in the night. It told her Japan would attack the United States and a great war would reach deep into Puerto Rico; every male between the ages of 18 and 45, it predicted, would soon be drafted.

If Mama had read or listened to the news, she might not have believed what she was told, for at that time nothing seemed farther from probability than an attack against the United States by Japan, a country considered too tiny and backward for the military experts to pay it much attention.

But almost exactly a year later, the sneak attack of December 7, 1941, bringing America into World War II, confirmed the accuracy of Mama's revelation. The fact is that while Mama was well-educated by Puerto Rican standards, she never paid any more attention to the radio or newspapers than Papa. They were both so deeply involved in their family and their work that they had little time for the news. Anyway, they got the important news in advance!

My mother never

knew any English, but one time I came home from school a few minutes behind my brother Salvador, and I found him shaking with laughter. "Listen to Mama!" he whispered.

Mama was in our living room saying something that sounded like jabbering at first, but I caught on as Salvador translated.

We had been studying English in school, and now Mama was speaking that language in a voice that sounded exactly like a cultured Englishman's. I don't remember now what she said; I do remember that Salvador was so amazed by the whole thing that he suddenly turned white and fainted, and at first my father thought that a spirit had possession of Salvador, too.

WHEN MAMA CAME OUT OF HER TRANCE, Salvador asked her in English: "Hello, Mama. What is for supper?"

Mama looked at him blankly, then burst out in Spanish: "Why don't you speak so I can understand you?"

She had no idea that she had just been speaking English.

Mama was a good mother and a tremendous help to Papa. Anyone looking at them could see how much they loved each other. He called himself "the Prince" and her "the Princess."

Mama was always so relaxed and happy-looking when she was with Papa.

Yet, we were not happy.

3

"BLACK" MAGIC VS. "WHITE" MAGIC

Early in his psychic career

Papa had dealings in what is called "black magic." A man asked him to put a curse on his enemy. Papa killed a black chicken, sprinkled the blood over the enemy's picture, and then drove a knife through the face. We heard that the man who had been hexed became violently ill.

But then Papa turned entirely to "white magic" and refused to hex anyone after that.

"The good spirits must help us drive away the bad spirits," he used to say. "There is no need to deal in destruction. It is better to build up than to tear down."

What a confused mixture of truth and lies! What a horrible deception, my friend!

We cannot fight demons using demons!

NONE OF US IS ANY MATCH FOR SATAN when we fight with his tools or on his terms! We cannot wage war against hell using the tactics of hell! Like my father, we just find ourselves swept into evil deceptions — closing our eyes to the evil compromises required of us.

Deep in his heart my father knew that he was not doing good. He felt great doubt and pangs of conscience as he went deeper and deeper into spiritism.

But he rationalized it away — just as all of us can do so easily. And he wasted an entire lifetime, seemingly fighting evil spirits, but instead just getting deeper and deeper involved with them — I remember that he claimed many of them were his friends!

Yet ... in later years he confessed to me that they were not *really* his friends. Numerous times after I became a Christian, he and I discussed the need for his salvation — and how he had to turn completely away from spiritism.

But he could not, he would tell me, his voice in a soft whisper. The spirits would kill him, he told me in complete seriousness. He had gone too far with them. He had seen too much. If he became a follower of Jesus Christ, they would take his life — rather than let him live and tell his terrible secrets. *Oh, my friend, imagine my anguish!*

My own father!

He believed that hell was his only eternal option.

THAT WAS A LIE STRAIGHT FROM SATAN! I told him so over and over. Yet, until the very end of his life, he was too frightened to turn his back on his dark spirit "friends."

How my father died is a remarkable story that I will share with you in another chapter, but I want you to understand that even as he practiced spiritism and claimed the friendship of the "good spirits," he knew that they were evil spirits and were not his true allies.

Instead, he was their terrified slave.

Early in his career, I believe, he accepted this horrible reality of having to consort with demonic forces because, he must have reasoned, the power they gave him was so immense!

As a result, he was so greatly respected by men!

And, he told himself, he did a great deal of good with that power. Sick people were healed ... even if my father found himself making deals with demons and forming alliances with darkness. Sad folks were cheered up by a chat with their "long-departed spouse" ... even if my mother had to give herself over to temporary possession by wild, evil spirits.

Curses were lifted. My father was an expert in this field. He could look you over and tell you that someone had put this or that hex on you. Then, he would tell you how to make stronger magic against the evil oppressing you. And he was very successful.

Many times people would come to us limping or in pain because of a curse. They would follow my father's prescription — sprinkling the blood of a black hen around their house and so forth — and they would get well.

But is this how you or I are supposed to wage spiritual warfare against the forces of evil coming against us?

Not at all. The Bible is clear that you and I can't have anything to do with any sort of magic! It's absolutely forbidden to us. The day after Israel's King Saul went to a medium and asked for the deceased Samuel to be summoned back, his kingdom was taken from him!

He died before the sun set again! Let us never forget what the Father allowed to happen to Saul — and to Israel.

Look at His warning in I Samuel 12:15: "If you rebel against the Lord's commandments and refuse to listen to him, then his hand will be as heavy upon you as it was upon your ancestors."

What commandments were those? How about I Samuel 12:20-22: "...make sure now that you worship the Lord with true enthusiasm, and that you don't turn your back on him in any way. Other gods can't help you. The Lord will not abandon his chosen people, for that would dishonor his great name. He made you a special nation for himself—just because he wanted to!"

What a wonderful promise!

And what warning: "... other gods can't help you!"

No, Satan *cannot help* us.

He is our enemy.

How are we to fight Satan?

First of all, none of us are any match for the devil as long as we make judgments based on our feelings — or if we look around at the problems around us.

He defeats us by showing us how terrible things are. He lies to us by showing how powerful he is and deceiving us into thinking that he is in control — and that we should join him by doubting God's goodness. That's his power at work in us. Fear and doubt *resist* faith.

Then, he tells us that he will take care of us.

Let's look at how he may be trying to weasel his way into your life. Money woes? Personal problems? A loved one in trouble?

Haven't you ever had that nagging thought to just rebuke God — and Satan promises that he'll make things better for you. After all, just look at all the wicked people around you having great fun and not troubled by Satan at all.

Well, as I just got through telling you: *None of us is any match for Satan as long as we make judgments based on our feelings — or if we look around at the problems he creates around us*.

How can anybody ignore the storm Satan is building all about us?

LOAD UP ON GOD'S PROMISES! Pack them into your memory. Jot them on your notepads. Hang them on your refrigerator door. Strict followers in the Old Testament said that we were to hang them from our doors, attach them to our sleeves and dangle them from our foreheads. Today some devout Jews wear little boxes which are filled with Bible verses.

I don't suggest that you do that, but hold onto God's promises.

Which promises?

How about I John 4:4, "Greater is he that is in you than he that is in the world"? Now, that's powerful! In times of doubt or testing, repeat it to yourself. Scribble it on a notecard. Send it to your spouse with a pretty card reminding him or her of your love. Hang it from your car's rear-view mirror.

Why?

Because you want to constantly remind yourself of the truth of God's absolute power over Satan. That way, you'll be undefeatable the next time depression or self-doubt or insecurity or money worries set in.

AH, NICKY, YOU MAY SAY, that's just a positive-thinking trick — and it's worldly.

No way! Jesus practiced it! When Satan tempted Him in the wilderness, Jesus threw Scriptures at him — destroying his arguments each time. *What did Satan try to seduce Jesus with?* Materialism. Greed. Power.

And the Lord shot him down bang, *bang, **bang***.

Armed with Scripture, you can get really bold and tell Satan where to go! What do you think Jesus was saying when Peter scoffed at the idea of Jesus being crucified soon? The Lord told him to quit that! In no uncertain terms, Jesus said: *"Get thee behind me, Satan!"*

So, this is not mere positive thinking, my friend.

We're in a spiritual war. I want you to take Ephesians 6:12 very seriously: "For we are not fighting against people made of flesh and blood, but against persons without bodies — the evil rulers of the unseen world, those mighty satanic beings and great evil princes of darkness who rule this world; and against huge numbers of wicked spirits in the spirit world."

And this is just a very basic way to begin fighting back effectively.

King David wrote in his Psalm 119:11: "Thy word have I hid in my heart that I may not sin against thee."

You need to do the same.

MAKE DAILY BIBLE READING a consistent part of your life. Start your day off reading something good from the Bible. Don't know where to start? Then, check the day of the month. Is it the 2nd? Or the 3rd? Or the 15th? Then read the corresponding chapter in Psalms or Proverbs or Matthew or Acts. Since those last two only have 28 chapters, on the 29th, 30th or 31st, read the entire book of II John, III John or Jude. Or have fun with the book of Philippians. It's full of great encouragement!

Get an easy-to-understand translation if the traditional thees, thous and whetherfores of the *King James Version* is gobbledegook to you. I recommend *The Living Bible* from Tyndale House publishers. It's great for light reading. For more intensive study, you might want to switch to the *Amplified Bible,* the *New American Standard* translation or one of the interesting paraphrases by Barclay or Phillips — all available in your local Christian bookstore.

AND AS YOU FILL YOUR MIND with the words of Almighty God, you're not dabbling in mere positive thinking — a humanistic half-truth which, I might add, won't really work without the power of the Lord working within you.

When you fill your heart and mind with Scripture, you're taking seriously your Christian life. II Timothy 3:16 says: "The whole Bible was given to us by inspiration from God and is useful to teach us what is true and to make us realize what is wrong in our lives; it straightens us out and helps us do what is right. "

Once Jesus told people who wanted to argue Scripture with him: "Your error is caused by your ignorance of the Scriptures and of God's power!" (See Matthew 22:29!)

By encouraging your spirit with the truths of God's promises to you, you're not doing anything magical, either. Your brain power isn't believing anything into existence. You are merely fortifying your tender, human spirit with the armor of truth!

You are reminding yourself that God is the winner, not the devil. Satan's doom, despair and defeat are just lies — flaming darts thrown at you to steal your joy and get you to surrender. He'd love for you to do that — give up in discouragement. *What a great tactic!*

After all, here you are, completely defended by the Almighty Creator — whom Satan cannot pretend to defeat — and protected by God's mighty angels, who have already beaten Satan and kicked him out of heaven. Yet, Satan would like you to walk out into the open with your hands in the air in surrender!

WHEN UNDER ASSAULT, MY FRIEND, here's another marvelous fistful of truth to hurl back at the devil: "The Lord is my light and my salvation; whom shall I fear?" (Psalm 27:1). Or how about Proverbs 18:10: "The Lord is a strong fortress. The godly run to him and are safe."

I Peter 5:8 says Satan roams about like a roaring lion looking for whomever he may devour. Well, when he comes prowling around *ROAR* the Word of God back at him! He is persistent and may not scoot out like a little scaredy-cat, but he'll know you mean business.

Why does Satan hate us so? Because we have what he wanted so desperately. He wanted to be mighty and powerful in heaven. Actually, he wanted to take over.

Instead, he lost it all. He was thrown out of paradise — banished from the presence of the loving, mighty Creator of All. Then the Father created humans and chose us to be joint heirs with Jesus, seated with Him in heaven.

That made Satan furious!

IT MADE HIM INSANELY AND HORRIBLY JEALOUS! So, he fills our minds with horrible lies full of defeat and despair. He tells us that our prayers do no good, that we're supposed to wallow in sin and poverty and unhappiness — and that God hates us.

But he knows the truth.

And he realizes that if you figure it out, it will set you free. When the brilliance of the Gospel of Jesus Christ shines in your darkness, all the evil lies are exposed as the falsehoods that they always were. And like a cockroach caught in the kitchen light, Satan scurries away into the darkness, filled with humiliation, fear and ... yes, vengeance.

So, that's why he keeps coming back.

That's why we have to be able to do battle with him.

And your first lesson in spiritual warfare is simple: fill your mind with the promises of your heavenly Father.

You're well protected, *but you need to know all about it!*

4

SON OF SATAN

A man from a sugar plantation

near Humacao one day came dragging up the road to our house with listless eyes and a greenish-yellow color to his skin. He said he had been feeling sick for two months and the doctor didn't know what was wrong. During the service Mama began to look so much like this man it was frightening; even her face looked yellowish and drawn. Papa finally told him to dig under the northeast corner of his house.

"You will find seven chicken bones tied to a coffin nail," Papa said. "Burn it all in a fire so hot the iron melts, and the curse that has been laid upon you will be destroyed."

Two days later this man came back leading a goat. He looked 100 percent younger and healthier. He said to Papa: "The bones were there as you said! I followed your instructions and the curse is gone. Please accept this goat as my gift for this miracle."

MY PAPA'S REPUTATION SPREAD even to the United States. One day a woman came to our house who said she had flown from New York to see Señor Cruz. This woman was very pale and haggard. She said she had met someone from Puerto Rico who told her about my father's powers.

"I don't believe in spirits," this American woman told my father, "but I wanted to see what a healer looks like. The Lord knows, no doctor in New York can find out what's wrong with me, and I certainly don't expect you to."

"Sit down," said my father. "I will tell you about yourself."

The woman laughed nervously. "If you can tell very much about me, you must have a good spy system."

"No," said my father. "You do not believe. I will make you believe. I will go to where you came from and describe it to you."

PAPA CLOSED HIS EYES. THERE WAS A SILENCE. Then he began to speak slowly. "You do not come from New York, but from a town near New York. You live on a street with many leafy trees. There is an iron fence in front of your house. Someone else lives there with you — two people. Your mother sits in a wheelchair. Your husband walks with a slight limp. He is worried. He is thinking about a very big company that makes telephones and cables…"

Papa stopped speaking because at that moment the visitor turned white and fainted. When she revived, her eyes were wide. "My husband owns a lot of stock in AT&T," she whispered, "and he was talking yesterday about selling some of it. How could you know?"

"The spirits show me many things," said Papa. "One thing they show me is why you are ill. A twisted spirit has you in his power. Would you like deliverance?"

Now the woman was sobbing. "I came here to ridicule," she said, "but I will do anything in my power to be well. Please help me!"

Papa stood up and laid his big hands on the woman's head. He closed his eyes. "Twisted one, be gone!"

Again the woman sobbed, this time in joy. "I feel free!" she said. "For the first time in years, I feel free."

When she left, this woman tried to hand Papa some money but he would not take it. He often refused to take payment for his services. But many people left gifts in gratitude — money, eggs, chickens, pigs, calves, sometimes a goat or even a cow.

PAPA TOLD FORTUNES, TOO. I suppose he inherited many of his powers from his mother, who used to tell fortunes and heal the sick on the Puerto Rican island of Vieques where Papa was raised. Although she could not read or write, Mama would tell expectant mothers what kind of babies they would have, and she was more accurate than the doctors or nurses in predicting the time of birth.

I cannot doubt that my father had psychic powers. But neither can I forget two other things about him.

Papa would become possessed

by a spirit he could not control. I remember once he grabbed my youngest brother, Felix. Papa put a rope around the little boy's neck and started to hang him from the limb of a tree.

It took the combined fury of Mama and my brothers and me to bring Papa back to his senses and save little Felix from strangulation.

Ironically, Felix was the baby, the one that Papa and Mama dearly loved — when they were themselves. If he had killed Felix, Papa would have been beside himself with grief.

Papa's children were important to him.

That's why it was so hard for him to accept there was one son he could not help.

BEFORE PAPA MET MY MOTHER, he had married and become father of three children on the Caribbean island of Vieques. His son Angelin sometimes acted very strangely. Once he ran away from home and was found by farmers on the other side of the island — completely naked, babbling, and fighting like a wild animal. Sometimes Angelin beat his head so hard against a wall, and became so wild that Papa had to tie him up.

Papa himself had had fits like that in his teens. It was this, in fact, that helped steer Papa into witchcraft. When Papa was about 17, he believed he had learned how to control the spirit that used to come over him and make him act like a madman. Through his 78 years he delivered many sufferers from similar maladies.

But nothing he did helped my half-brother Angelin.

Then one day, Angelin went into a Christian revival service. When the invitation was given he went forward and knelt down — and was delivered completely from this inexplicable problem. Today Angelin is a happy Christian.

Looking at him, you would never think he had once been subject to these strange fits. Jesus brought Angelin the complete healing that Papa couldn't deliver.

Papa had some strong medicine. But Jesus was stronger.

Unfortunately, we did not know anything about that, yet.

When my mother

called me "Satan's son" that day when I was eight years old, how close to the truth was she?

During my first eighteen years it often seemed like two beings were struggling with each other deep inside me. Part of me wanted to do what was right — and part of me hated authority and goodness. Part of me loved my strong father and my lovely mother and my sister Carmen and all sixteen of my brothers. How proud of them I felt, sometimes, when we were all together! But another part of me came to hate them so much that I was almost happy when at age 15, my father put me on a plane to New York in the hopes that I would straighten up.

I was delighted to leave them far behind.

YOU CAN TALK ABOUT MIXED-UP KIDS, but particularly after my mother denounced me and let me know how she truly felt about me being a curse on the family, I was more mixed up than anyone I can think of. As a rule my brothers liked school, learned fast, were gentle and polite, a lot like my parents.

I was the odd one. I hated school and my teachers. I loved vicious, practical jokes. I grated against people like sandpaper.

Once when I was little I threw a rock down our hill and it bounced off the ground by a mango tree and knocked over a little girl, Maria, who was playing there in her yard with her sister. I ducked out of sight and no one knew who threw the rock. Maria was bleeding and was unconscious for a while. I had the funniest feeling when I heard people talking about her. I was scared, but something inside me felt excited and satisfied when I thought maybe I'd killed her.

I used to steal from Mama. Papa caught me at it once. After that I always watched to see that no one was around when I took coins or bills out of the basket where Mama thought nobody knew she kept them. I never took enough at one time so she would notice it, and I got a big thrill out of fooling her and outwitting Papa that way.

AS I GOT BIGGER I STOLE MORE — sometimes several dollars a day. One time I bought a watch with this easily acquired money, another time a BB gun. With this I like to hide where no one could see me and pepper the legs of unsuspecting passersby. I also loved to wound small animals and watch them bleed, then die. Of course, I kept such things as the watch and gun hidden away from the sight of Mama and Papa.

But one night, I got caught.

Papa saw me with my hand in Mama's purse. I tried to run, but he caught me by the back of my neck.

"I hate you!" I screamed at him.

Suddenly, he was shaking me like a rag doll.

"You will never talk to your Papa like that, you little thief," he snarled. Throwing me under his arm like a sack of potatoes, he strode outside into the darkness and toward his pigeon coop — a smelly shed where his dirty pets nested.

Fumbling in the dark with the lock, "Thief!" he swore. "Filthy thief! Get inside, Little Bird. Stay in the dark with the other animals until you learn your lesson!"

Roughly he thrust me into the swirling chaos of the frightened birds.

Surely he could not have known my utter terror.

Hysterical, I tried to shield my face. It was as if I had awakened in hell. In the oppresively hot darkness, I spun around and around, fighting to breathe as I beat off their flapping wings, their pecking beaks, their slamming bodies. Insane with fright, I hammered and kicked on the walls — screaming until I was hoarse — *to no avail.*

It seemed forever

before Papa yanked open the door and pulled me out by my shirt collar. "Next time, you'll think twice before you steal or sass your father," he snarled.

Trembling, I sought comfort from him. But he refused to hold me close or hug me. "Go get cleaned up, Little Bird. And get to bed. No supper for you."

Desperately alone, I cried myself to sleep that night. New, vivid nightmares were filled with vengeful birds trying to peck my eyes out. So, this was what a Little Bird was, I wept to myself in the lonely darkness.

And I continued to steal — but more carefully now — perhaps in defiance of my Papa.

But mostly, I liked the things that stolen cash bought me. Sometimes I would steal a dime or a quarter and get a ticket to the movie theater in Las Piedras. I loved to watch Tarzan of the Apes swinging through far-off jungles that reminded me of our own rain forest a few miles away. And I was especially fond of cowboy heroes — Roy Rogers, the Lone Ranger, and El Lobo, the Latin outlaw who could always outwit his enemies with a fast horse and a good gun.

One of the things I bought with the money I stole was a bicycle. That really made me somebody. I kept it away from our house, and when Mama and Papa learned I had a bicycle, I invented a long story about how another boy had loaned it to me, and they believed me.

WITH MY BIKE I COULD DO all kinds of things. One day I was coasting along a dirt road between Las Piedras and Humacao when I passed a little kid carrying two bottles of Coke. I reached down and snatched one bottle away from him. This little boy spun around to see what was happening, stubbing his toe, and dropped the other bottle on a rock. As I went around a bend in the road I could see this kid standing there crying, and that sight made me feel even better than getting a free Coke. I could picture how he felt, and the licking he would probably get when he got home with no money and no Coke. Now it hurts me to think of it.

But then it made me laugh with devilish glee.

5

MY VICIOUS
NEW FAMILY

I was exiled to New York

at age 15. My dad finally could not handle me. So, he took me to the airport, gave me a $10 bill, handed my plane ticket to the attendant, and wished me a better life than I had started in Puerto Rico.

"Goodbye, Little Bird," he said.

I did not expect to ever see him or my beautiful island in the Caribbean again. I arrived in New York City an angry wild animal. Although I was supposed to live with one of my brothers, Frank, I ran off immediately. I was hypnotized by the evil possibilities of this immense metropolis.

Soon I fell in with a vicious bunch of street hoods. But my fancy-walking, mean-talking Mau Maus didn't act like outcasts. They stole whatever they needed through burglary, intimidation, outright extortion and, occasionally, armed robbery. *They dressed sharp, though.* And they stuck together.

I fought my way to the top. Every time my fist thudded against a skull, I got a tremendous charge. When we were fighting with knives, it felt good to ... *hurt people.*

It was a brutal city and I had to be tougher than anybody if I was going to be king of the streets, lord of the concrete jungle.

So, I was meaner than anybody. I survived when others died.

And I *always* won.

EVERY SO OFTEN SOME DIFFERENT THING comes back to me from those days of the gangs, and I wonder how I could have been the way I was.

Like my first armed robbery. Using a switchblade I'd taken in a fight, I robbed a kid walking home from a grocery store. I made an easy $19. It felt good — particularly my sheer power over the terrified kid. He would have done anything I said. I laughed in evil glee.

And I remember the night the Mau Maus let me join them. They had named themselves after a particularly blood-thirsty tribe of rebel Africans who had been making international headlines for their particularly brutal murders of anyone who encroached on their jungle. In black, leather jackets emblazoned with a crimson, double M, New York's Mau Maus swaggered down the Brooklyn streets, terrifying everyone who crossed their paths.

THAT NIGHT OF MY INITIATION, I had already made a name for myself at school. I'd fought and scrapped my way through class — tangling with everybody from the drug-dealing janitors to the angry principal who hid in his office. He had expelled me — unfairly, I believed — when I stopped a rape in one of my classes. *I didn't care.* School had been a joke — a hell-hole of drugs, violence and sexual intimidation. Very little learning took place. The gangs ruled — and I saw that I wanted to be a part of the real power on the streets and in the classroom: the most feared gang, the murderous Mau Maus.

I began hanging around their "gigs" — street parties. My blood raced as I watched the raucous violence of a good time, the open sex, the free-flowing liquor, the cocaine and marijuana available to members. I envied the boys my age who flashed their guns and beautiful knives. I listened with excitement as they told of enemies' horrible, tortured deaths.

"HEY, NICKY," CHALLENGED THE MAU MAU PRESIDENT the third night I hung around the edges of their orgy. "Nicky! We got another boy who wants to join the Mau Maus. You want to get initiated, too?"

"I'm ready," I laughed, swaggering. "I'm ready to fight. I'm just as tough as anybody here — and a better fighter than most of your guys."

"Good," said the president. "You watch. Then it'll be your turn."

What followed made my heart pump deliriously. A frightened 15-year-old stood against the wall as Carlos, the president, used him as a knife target. About 50 boys and girls hooted in eager excitement.

"I'm gonna turn around now," mocked Carlos, "and I'm gonna walk 20 steps. You stand right there. When I count 20, I'm gonna spin and throw this blade. If you flinch or duck, you're a coward. If you don't move even if the knife sticks you, you're a tough kid and can join the Mau Maus. Understand?"

Trembling, the boy nodded and tried to stand tall. As Carlos began to walk and count aloud, the crowd began to jeer: "Stick him, Carlos! Stick it through his eye. Make him bleed, man! Make him hurt!"

DESPERATELY TRYING TO BE BRAVE, the young target shrank against the wall — not daring to flinch. "Eighteen ... nineteen," called Carlos. The cold-blooded gang was wild in its frenzy. As Carlos spun around, the kid dropped to his knees, his arms around his head.

"No! No!" he pleaded.

The crowd was enraged. Angrily, Carlos yelled for two Mau Maus to grab the kid and make him stand up. "Chicken!" he spat, "I ought to kill you. I'm gonna cut your heart out and let you see it beat in my hand while you gasp your last chicken breath!"

"Kill him!" yelled the rabid mob.

"You know what we do to chickens?" Carlos held his knife under the boy's nose. "We clip their wings so they never fly again." And suddenly, Carlos thrust his knife into the boy's armpits — quickly, almost up to the hilt.

With blood pouring down the boy's shirt, the child collapsed into the floor, his hands flailing his ripped flesh, a crimson pool forming around him.

"Get him out of my face," yelled Carlos. "Where's Nicky?"

IT WAS MY TURN. BUT I WASN'T AFRAID. The sight of blood had exhilarated me. The excitement of the pain and stabbing and the screams of defeat throbbed through my mind. I stepped forward.

The savage crowd demanded more blood as Carlos looked me over. "We got another chicken?" he leered.

"Not me," I yelled. "I'll take on anybody here. Come on!"

Carlos laughed cruelly — then called out five names. Enormous teens twice my size crowded around me. One danced beside me, shadow boxing the air. Another tried to stare me down, snorting his hot, putrid breath into my upturned face. A heavily muscled weight-lifter removed his shirt and spat in my ear. The crowd roared.

"Here's your test," announced Carlos. "You don't move a muscle. You just stand there while these five guys kill you."

I didn't have a chance to protest. A kid with one ear missing loomed to my right as another boy slammed his fist into my kidney. The unexpected pain was excruciating. I tried to gasp for breath, but a blow to the stomach knocked the air out of me. I struggled to stand as I felt my nose crumble another another fist.

I FELT MYSELF FALLING, then someone holding me up by my hair as a foot slammed into my mouth. They all converged, turning me into a punching bag as I lost consciousness.

Sometime later, I became aware of somebody slapping me in the face and ordering me to stand up. I tried to focus my eyes, but could see nothing. Then I tasted my own blood.

And I went crazy. Lying in a big puddle of sticky blood, I began kicking and spinning around, striking out with my fists and feet.

Somebody grabbed me and pinned me to the floor.

"You're OK, Nicky!" Carlos was yelling. "You're in, man! We can use your kind, that's for sure." I felt him pressing something into my hand.

It was a .32-caliber pistol.

I gripped it and laughed to myself.

Now I was a Mau Mau.

Such memories.

What hellish days and nights. Like one evening when Nighthawk and Mingo and I were trying out a car we stole off the streets and drove past a guy we recognized as Little George, a member of the Forty-Niners. That was a small gang that had caught two Mau Maus three days before and burned their faces with acid.

Nighthawk was driving. He slammed on the brakes and Mingo and I jumped out and shoved Little George into the car before he knew what was happening. We held him and used our knives and cigarettes for a while to make him jump and yell, while Nighthawk drove all over the deserted streets of Brooklyn and Harlem.

At last we decided to dump Little George. Nighthawk was hitting about 65 on the Harlem River Drive when Mingo opened the door and we pushed Little George out so he bounced off a concrete abutment.

NOW I GET SICK TO MY STOMACH when I think about it. But while we were doing things like that, it was more a thrill than anything else. I felt revved-up and filled — full as though I'd just had a big meal or a girl, and we sang songs all the way home.

And the rumbles … the fights between gangs. Perhaps they were "recreational" — for we loved the excitement of hand-to-hand warfare. But it was more than that. New York City was divided up into little zones. Confrontation would break out when one gang moved in on another's turf.

We were a little world — with borders and war machines — and innocent citizens getting hurt in the unending fighting. *We loved it.*

One night, we took on a feared black gang, the Bishops. Our ambassadors met and set up the plan. We would fight it out at 10 p.m. on the playground of Public School 67. *It was going to be bloody, I knew.* My new best friend, Israel, told me to bring my revolver and anything else I had.

We began gathering at 8:30. Many of us had guns. Others wielded baseball bats, boards with spikes hanging out at the top, sharpened bicycle chains — and lots of knives. Carlos had a two-foot bayonet. A kid named Hector had a sawed-off shotgun.

WE SPLIT UP. ONE MAIN BODY would meet the Bishops head on. Others would wade in from the sides when we needed reinforcements. Others still would wait and cut off the Bishops' retreat, ambushing them if they tried to run — or jumping them from behind if it looked bad for us.

People died that night. In the 10 minutes of gory frenzy, we lost boys and so did the Bishops.

I remember amid the blood and the excitement and the wail of police sirens how I leveled my gun at one fleeing kid, pulling the trigger twice and feeling my heart race as the small boy stumbled and fell to the ground.

He was crawling away as Israel dragged me into an alley. "We gotta go!" he was shouting. "The cops are here, man!"

As 200 Mau Maus and Bishops scattered, the police waded into a war scene. Young bodies lay on the ground. Some would never move again. *I felt good.*

I had seen blood flow. I had shot someone — maybe even killed him. And we had gotten away.

Israel put his arm around me as we puffed a marijuana joint: "You're OK, Nicky," he exclaimed for all to hear. "I been looking for somebody like you for a long time. When I'm in a fight, I want you there!"

He roared with mirth.

"Yeah," he yelled. "We're both just alike, man! We're both nuts!"

SOME DAYS LATER, I took part in a particularly memorable armed robbery. It was an all-night cafe run by an old man and his wife.

I remember the terror on their faces.

I can still see the horror in their eyes as I threatened the old woman and scooped the cash out of the register.

We hooted in derision as the old man clutched his chest, his face white.

He sank to his knees — apparently in mid-heart attack.

We all laughed as we ran away into the darkness.

Maybe it was that evening ... or another, when a bunch of the wilder, more blood-thirsty guys laid in wait in a dark alley — drinking and smoking dope. Suddenly, they spotted a prospective victim on the street. Sneaking up on her and throwing a blanket over her head, they beat her into unconsciousness, then dragged her up to the rooftops. There in the moonless night's darkness, laughing, drunk in their violence, they raped her over and over. When she regained consciousness, she began pleading with one boy in particular to stop.

But filled with drunken lust, the boy only laughed and announced that he wanted to assault her a second time. Striking a match to light his cigarette, he held the flame close to her face. Then his scream echoed through the dark alleys.

"Mom!" he shrieked. "Momma! No! No! *No!*" Suddenly he ran like a maniac and leaped to his death, plunging to the concrete below.

His mother was never the same. She was taken away to New York City's Bellvue Hospital psychiatric ward.

MANY TIMES I WAS CONSCIOUS of a horrible force that seemed to have me in its control. Somehow I knew that what I was doing was part of an evil design ... a wicked purpose far greater than my own — a vile purpose bent on death and destruction.

At such times I felt terrible fear.

Was it a curse?

Had my father hexed me?

Was my mother right — Did I have the mark of Satan on my heart? Was I the son of Lucifer? Was I doomed to burn in hell forever? I laughed at the prospect. If I had to go, *I would take many others with me!*

ON ONE OF THOSE OCCASIONS I almost killed my brother Gene. He was a wonderful fellow. He's only a year older than me, and we had become very close.

He was a real big brother to me. He had a good job and he had given me some money and taken me shopping with him at Macy's and Ohrbach's in Manhattan. We had a great time going through all the departments, watching the girls, and getting so many things that we left most of them to be delivered to Gene's apartment.

I remember I got two new pairs of shoes and a sharp jacket and Gene bought a necklace for his girlfriend, Lucia.

On the subway back I kidded Gene about the necklace. "You give her too much," I said. "Girls are for kicks. What's the good of giving them all these things? Love 'em and split is my philosophy."

I was partly kidding, but more than half serious. The truth is, I resented the way Gene lived. He was always courteous, polite, and bright in school, and he treated girls like they would break if you handled them rough. I didn't, and it made me mad that he did.

"Lucia will like this," said Gene, patting the pocket where he had put the necklace.

"I can think of girls who would give you more than she will — cheaper!" I said.

Gene changed the subject, and nothing much happened until we got to Broadway and Lafayette, where we had to change subway trains and catch the D train back to Brooklyn.

It seemed like a long wait as we stood by the tracks waiting for the D train to arrive. I wasn't thinking about anything in particular when the lights came around a bend in the subway tunnel.

SUDDENLY THE MOST OVERWHELMING FEELING came over me, an impulse to push Gene in front of the train charging down the tunnel toward us. It was a feeling of evil, of anger, of hate — pure and simple. The horrible thought took possession of my mind:

The subway needs a victim. Your brother is to be victim. Offer the sacrifice NOW before the moment is gone!

I could picture myself pushing Gene in front of the train, the roaring cars, the flashing wheels, the mangled body, the flying blood. Gene — with his moral superiority — gone from my life!

He is standing there waiting. NOW!

I moved toward him. His back was turned to me, oblivious. I felt that the one thing I had to do was push him over the edge of the subway platform, watch his body hurtle beneath the grinding wheels, get rid of him forever. The feeling was a blinding, driving force inside me. My hands shot out like pistons.

But there was a spark of warmth in my heart that was not quite out. This was my brother, who had always been so good and generous to me!

"Gene!" I screamed.

GENE WHIRLED AROUND, leaped to one side as I fought to keep by body from doing what my brain had been commanding. Alarm filled his face as he saw mine. My thoughts must have been written in my eyes, for he turned white.

"Nicky!" he gasped. "What's the matter? What are you doing?"

The D train opened its doors, let out its passengers, shut its doors again, and took off into the darkness as we stood there looking at each other.

"I don't know," I said. "Something must have come over me."

Gene's face crumpled up and he began to cry as he realized what I had nearly done. "Oh, Nicky!" he sobbed. "What is wrong with you?"

I didn't know — *except that I had nearly lost control of everything decent and human that was left inside of me.*

6

TOO YOUNG TO DIE

Many times

when I was in my room in Brooklyn I felt angry, desperately lonely, depressed. I had risen to the presidency of the Mau Maus. But it wasn't enough. While part of me gloated over my success in crime and rebellion, part of me felt guilty and sad and hopeless.

I heard again and again the accusations of my mother's voice: *Son of Satan, child of devil! Mark of beast on your heart! Curse on our family! Hand of Lucifer on your life!*

At such times I often felt like selling out completely to the devil. I had come close to it. I think now that there is a point in anyone's life that, once crossed, it is, humanly speaking, impossible to go back. At those times I was desperately close to that line. I could practically hear a sinister voice saying: *Give up. Let me take over. I promise you more fun than you can dream of. Why don't you quit fighting and let me take control?*

I'm stubborn. I guess I was 99 percent Satan's, but there was one tiny part left, holding back. I still held on to a few shreds of decency and self-respect. I wasn't willing to give myself over completely to anyone.

I could also sense, from little things they hinted at, that many of the guys in the Mau Maus were feeling the same kind of struggle. We lived so close to hell all the time, it's a wonder any of us escaped total destruction. But bad as we were, some of us held out against giving in completely to the Evil One.

SO WHEN I GOT DEPRESSED I would often puff marijuana and take all kinds of pills and uppers and downers until I had drowned out reality and drifted into troubled dreams. Sometimes I'd knock myself out with wine or rum. And sometimes when nothing else worked I got so desperate I pounded the wall with my fists until my knuckles bled, or banged my head against the wall until I was unconscious. I was like a caged animal, desperate to get out but not knowing how. I felt evil and guilty and helpless.

I sought relief in every pleasure that occurred to me.

But nothing satisfied.

Except violence. *It was our religion.* I sought it out. I gloried in our battlefield exploits. I remember one fight when we captured one of the rival Phantom Lords.

We were having a great time out on the sidewalk — stripping his pants off of him and hooting our derision as he fled, bare-bottomed and bloody into the night. But as we laughed, his friends quietly surrounded us. In mid-chuckle, I was slammed to the sidewalk, kicked in the skull by a Phantom Lord wearing sharp metal cleats.

A lead pipe caught me along the side of the head as the boy with the cleats stomped on my legs and hips.

I woke up on the floor of my apartment where Israel and Manny had dragged me. I was a mass of bruises and bloody cuts. Painfully, we peeled my clothing out of the wounds. In agony, I stood in the public shower down the hall.

Then, I staggered, naked, down the corridor as the other tenants gawked and whispered.

I collapsed into my bed — thinking of the Phantom Lord we had forced to run down the street without pants.

Somehow, he had gotten me back, I knew.

AND I FELT THE HORROR of watching friends fall. Manny, died one dark Christmas Day — in my arms. Shortly after he was born, his unwed mother had placed him carefully in a garbage can. Then, she had climbed up onto a rooftop and set herself on fire with a gallon of gasoline. As her baby screamed for her, she expired in flames. Manny was raised by relatives — and was strangely sensitive and tender for a gang member. He was gentle with his friends — but could be just as savage as any other of the Mau Maus when the situation called for it.

On Christmas morning, we were jumped by the Bishops as we sat laughing and talking at a lunch counter. There was a nasty feud going —

Manny had been threatened by a Bishop that we'd jumped and burned badly.

Now, we dived out a side door, but the Bishops were everywhere. Laughing and yelling, I butted my head into a Bishop's stomach and grappled with a knife-wielding enemy. Repeatedly, he jabbed me — but I wrestled away and bellered for Manny to follow as I tore down the street.

Then, I turned and saw.

They had him down. They were kicking and stabbing and punching and glancing around for the cops. Like a madman, I raced to his rescue.

TAUNTING ME, THEY SCATTERED. I knelt in pain and held my friend's head to my chest. On my knees, I rocked him gently. "Manny," I whispered, "it'll be OK, man."

When he tried to speak, all I could hear was a gurgle in his lungs. He blew little blood bubbles with his lips. I yanked off his jacket and saw the multiple, deep stab wounds.

"Manny," I screamed, "don't die, man! Don't die!"

Then there was the soft hiss of his last breath. His head rolled limply against my chest. I stared at his unblinking eyes.

"Manny!" I screamed in the filth and the blood of the street. "No! Manny!"

A woman walked out into the street and screamed. There was the distant sound of a police siren. I panicked. I'd been arrested so many times that I'd be blamed. Jumping up, I let Manny's body fall to the pavement.

And I ran — although I, too, was badly wounded.

Alone in my tenement apartment, I bandaged my cuts and screamed my hatred and my fury. I pounded the walls. I put my revolver to my head and almost took my own life.

But I stopped short of pulling the trigger.

NO, INSTEAD, I WOULD AVENGE HIM, I hissed to myself. The Bishops would pay. Many would die. *I made good on my promise.* But it did not help the aching hurt. Manny had died in my arms. Without love. Without *hope.* And I'd had to leave his body out on the dirty concrete, like a dead rat somebody had discarded.

My depression grew. Out on the street, I grew tired of eating the same greasy food and watching the vermin-infested buildings deteriorate. Everything was filthy and falling apart. The only girls around were street prostitutes. The grown women were screaming winos, kicking their filthy kids out into the sidewalk where their loser fathers were sitting around playing cards and dominos and drinking beer.

ONE DAY I WAS IN THE SUBWAY STATION near Prospect Park, waiting for a train that seemed to take forever to arrive. As I stood there leaning against the dirty wall, the most awful wave of loneliness and emptiness swept over me. I thought of all the mean things I had done, of my home far away, of the future — what future?

Would I end up like the Mau Maus who had been buried recently, killed in a gang war, or in prison for the rest of my life? I watched the homosexuals hustling out on the train platform and the drug addicts hiding in the shadows and I wondered: What was the point to life, anyway?

Was I cursed to be Satan's son forever?

I trembled in anger. Why was the stupid subway train so late? Why did *everything* in my life always turn out so **WRONG**?

All of a sudden, I smelled something burning. I felt something warm — hot — on my hip. I looked down and saw smoke coming out of my pocket.

My matches had burst into flame.

How? I hadn't been smoking.

There was no earthly reason for those matches to ignite — but they had caught fire. My mind flashed back to the strange things my parents had sometimes done in Puerto Rico. No connection, I told myself, but I couldn't deny all that I had seen as a youngster. Was this strange fire a reminder that I was Satan's son?

I could never explain why those matches caught fire.

I still can't.

LITTLE BIT WAS A CUTE, CURLY-HAIRED KID about ten years old who kept trying to join the Mau Maus. Everyone in the gang laughed at the idea, of course—the kid was even smaller than his age. We threw him out of our meeting place time after time, but he was always hanging around and would sneak along behind us when we had a rumble and try to fight on our side.

One night when the Mau Maus were fighting the Bishops, a gang of Phantom Lords showed up behind us. Outnumbered, the Mau Maus had to use an escape route we had reserved for real emergencies. It led over rooftops for a whole block and to get to the last rooftop we had to clear a terrific distance between buildings.

A tough fighter named Nighthawk and I were the first across, and everyone in the gang made it to safety. As everyone was rushing down the fire escape, I took a last look back and I saw three Phantom Lords racing across the rooftop behind us — with Little Bit in front of them.

I yelled, "Little Bit! Don't."

It was too late. Little Bit made a beautiful try. He raced across that roof and sailed across the empty space between two buildings.

Almost.

HE FELL JUST SHORT. His pathetic little hands clawed at the cornice for a moment and then he was gone, and his horrible scream as he fell ended in a sickening thud in the alley below. No one in the Mau Maus said much about Little Bit after that, but the next time a little kid tried to follow us, we got out our knives, if we had to, to scare him away.

Little Bit was attracted by the thrills of being in a street gang. He had no idea what he was getting sucked into.

Death.

A spiral downward.

When I attended the funeral, I was met by his screaming, hate-filled mother.

"You!" she shrieked at me and the other Mau Maus standing in respectful silence. "Get out of here! How dare you defile this place? Get out of here, you dirty scum!"

I left.

And I knew she was right.

I KNEW I WAS GOING STRAIGHT DOWNHILL fast, but I wasn't willing or able to turn around.

As the gang wars grew in intensity, I became a sort of cult figure in the newspapers. We began terrorizing the theater district of Manhattan — the rich people coming out of the show were easy targets.

And it seemed as if New York City were aflame. We were in all the newspapers and magazines as the youth street gangs declared war on the police. I had six brothers living in New York City — who also had been sent to the big city by my dad. After I had been jailed repeatedly, they contacted my father.

I scoffed at the idea of a rural Puerto Rican witchdoctor helping me. Even a court psychiatrist had thrown up his hands in defeat at my situation, telling me that I was headed straight for prison, the electric chair and hell.

AFTER I HAD BEEN IN THE NEWSPAPERS several times, the police began lying in wait for me. When I didn't have my gang members to protect me, they would sweep in, nab me and take me into custody for hours of questioning.

One time, they really got to me — but still I didn't talk. Three days in the middle of winter, they kept me naked into a solitary cell with all the windows open. It completely freaked me out, not because it was so brutally cold, but because it somehow reminded me of the night my father had thrown me in with the pigeons. I caught a terrible cold and was a screaming basket case by the time they came to get me, but I did not inform. I would not tell them anything.

I DIDN'T KNOW IT, BUT THEY were under tremendous pressure from politicians in the city and state governments to solve the problem of the youth gangs terrorizing New York's streets. The police had devoted enormous time to infiltrating the Mafia, but they had no idea of what to do with us.

We were too young to infiltrate. When they sent stool pigeons to try to join us, we caught them every time. None of them lived to tell their tales.

The police began using a favorite stunt on me — one that had ridded them of other vicious gangleaders. After one of their long interrogations, they would drop me off — disarmed, of course — in the middle of some vicious rival gang's turf.

They figured I was a dead man.

The other gangs hated me, the head of the Mau Maus. They were more than delighted to cooperate with the cops and try to murder me in the street. *But I always got away*. The only reason I made it was that I was a *survivor*.

I fought my way home.

One time, cornered by a rival gang, I made a desperate dash down into the subway. The train was already pulling out — I was a dead man.

But I could not give up.

I leaped onto the back of the last car and hung on for dear life as gunshots and curses rang out in the darkness.

I laughed. I was indestructible!

Or was I?

ONE DEPRESSING AFTERNOON, I caught sight of a child's balloon bouncing along in the gutter. For some reason, it grabbed my imagination.

I strained to watch it — then began to run along the littered sidewalk, cheering it on. The balloon bounced and rolled along the street, somehow not exploding. It's strange how an inanimate object caught my fancy like that, but I began to get excited. All around it were papers and trash, also blown in the cold wind, but snagging on broken bottles and beer cans. Yet, the little balloon survived!

Towering on each side were the dismal concrete and steel tenements of our Brooklyn hell. Lounging on the stoops and lying hung-over in the doorways were the debris of corrupted humanity, but bobbing along in the sunshine was a free, red balloon — untouched by the ugly reality of our inescapable prison.

What was it about this child's toy that held my attention and filled with me with such joy and hope? I can't explain it. I knew the balloon couldn't survive — but there it was! It was so delicate, so clean, tender and pure ... defying the ugliness of our manmade hell.

"Maybe it will make it," I began thinking. "Maybe it can get all the way down the block and be blown free into the park. *Maybe it has a chance after all.*" I was almost praying for it!

But as I rounded a corner, a police van rolled up out of nowhere. I ducked into an alley and watched in horror as my little balloon rolled under the van's front tire and deflated with a tiny "pop."

Squatting in the filth, I was suddenly filled with dejection. I buried my face in my hands.

Nothing could survive in this hell.

Nobody.

MY NIGHTS BEGAN TO BE FILLED with nightmares. I was swallowed up with terrible, gnawing fears.

I dreamed of my father, chained in a cave. He had teeth like a wolf and his body was covered with sparse, mangy fur. He barked pathetically — and I wanted to go up and comfort him.

But I was afraid. He would bite me, I knew.

He always had when I tried to get close to him.

And then there were the dreams of the pigeons. My brother Luis would ride off into the sky on the back of a great bird, but I would be engulfed in a cloud of the squawking, thrashing, pecking pigeons. Every time I would break free of them, I would see Luis soaring in the sky.

I began to fear sleep.

Every time that I nodded off, I would be confronted by my snarling father.

Papa, the exorcist

My life of crime had to end,

my brothers decided. At age 17, I was shaming the family name and flirting daily with death. I was on a one-way trip to the electric chair.

My brother Louis pleaded with Papa to come to New York and talk some sense into me. Papa flew to the city and met with my brothers, Gene, Frank, Efraim, Salvador and my sister, Carmen, who was 15 and staying with one of my brothers. They made plans to exorcise demons that Papa believed were tormenting me and causing me to do such bad things.

My brothers and sister tracked me down to the filthy apartment where I lived in the Fort Greene housing project of Brooklyn. They took me to a darkened apartment that my father had prepared specially for an *espiritista* exorcism. He had black candles lit and strange incense and other *espiritista* paraphernalia that I recognized from my childhood.

"I SENSE FIVE EVIL SPIRITS IN YOU," declared my father, motioning to my brothers to grab me and pin me to the floor. I fought, but they were too strong. "Five demons. That is why you are so delinquent! Today, I shall cure you!"

What followed was a horror story scenario that only those who grow up in such evil can truly understand. A great, loathsome spirit filled the room, telling us all secrets of our lives—and guiding Papa as he brutally attempted to banish the repulsive forces from my soul.

The spirit declared that it was my grandfather on my mother's side.

"I'm suffering for you," the spirit told me. Then it began to describe everything I was doing, life with the gangs and details of robberies we had committed. I got scared.

"I want you to go back to Puerto Rico," the spirit told me. Then, it told me that it knew I was carrying a gun — and that it could make me use the gun to kill myself if it wanted to.

I did not run out of the room only because I greatly feared my father — and believed that he would curse me if I fled. But under my breath, I swore as the evil spirit spoke and as my father prayed and commanded phantasms to leave his violent, rebellious eighth son.

Then the exorcism became physical. My father, then my sister began to hit me with their fists. But for the first time in months, I did not fight back.

CHOKING ME UNTIL I COULD NOT BREATHE, slamming his fists against my aching ribs, my father exhausted himself.

It was 2:30 a.m. when he sat back — then proclaimed me clean of evil spirits. Suddenly, the lights went off in the apartment. The sink water turned on and the radio and TV burst into life. My brothers Frank and Salvador rushed into the room and said that upstairs, Carmen had suddenly become possessed. When we ran up to see, she was out of control. Her eyes were turned around backwards. She was cursing and calling me Satan.

Frank began calling on the spirits of our ancestors to deliver her. And, without warning, she was let go. I started laughing and mocking her. I know my father could see that his efforts had been for nothing.

"Nicky," he said softly. "You hurt. You are hurting so badly."

Then he looked down. "And I don't blame you."

It was an *apology*. He knew I'd had a hellish childhood.

He didn't expect to see me alive again — and he wanted me to know that he was sorry for failing to raise me right. "I hope it is not too late for you," he said, "but it will not be much longer until you will die."

I stared at him in shock. I was 17 years old. I was too young for *that.*

I RAN OUT THE DOOR AND ROBBED A SAILOR I found sleeping in the park. I was so angry — it didn't matter who it was. I had to take vengeance against somebody.

If indeed my father had cast out any evil spirits, seven more demons had returned in each of their places — nor did I want to be delivered.

Into the night air, I screamed my hatred for everything that my father symbolized. I was ashamed for my friends in the Mau Maus to see him or find out what he was: *a witchdoctor from Puerto Rico*. His idiotic religion was a shameful secret that I longed to just forget. I wanted no spirits bossing me around. I wanted no one making fun of me for my superstitions.

I would stand on my own.

Alone.

Vicious.

Undefeated.

BUT ALONE IN MY ROOM, I WAS DEVASTATED. I was worthless and I knew it.

I thought of the terrible pain I had caused so many people. I thought of Manny. And of Little Bit's mother. And of my own mother. *Son of Satan. Mark of Lucifer on your life.* The words echoed in my ears.

I was at the bottom.

I could sink no lower.

YET, I GUESS MY ENORMOUS PRIDE and stubbornness were part of the reason I hated David Wilkerson so much when I first laid eyes on him.

He had answers.

I was beyond answers. I only knew death.

And I was waiting for it to try to take me.

On a street in our Brooklyn slum, Wilkerson seemingly showed up out of nowhere, standing under a street light. Some man with him was tooting a trumpet and somebody else was waving an enormous American flag. Then Wilkerson began preaching at the top of his lungs.

My lieutenants and I moved easily to the front of the crowd as everybody moved out of my way.

I simply could not believe my eyes. Here, in the middle of the deadly Mau Maus' turf, in the dangerous Fort Greene project slums — where even the cops stuck close together and where a parked car got stripped in seconds — was a crazy man.

A country-bumpkin.

And he was apparently too naive to be scared of us.

8

I BEGAN TO PLAN HIS MURDER

The preacher was skinny,
so thin that it looked like he was going to fall over if he didn't stop yelling and waving that enormous Bible. He was wearing some foolish-looking country-preacher suit and trying to convert everybody to his religion.

I hated him instantly. Here was a witch completely dominated by a spirit absolutely opposite of everything I was.

I loved death. *He offered life.* I felt glee at the sight of other people's pain. *He offered healing to the hurting.*

His was a spirit of peace. But I was consumed with a spirit of war. *Mayhem. DESTRUCTION!* — and he wanted me to be like him — *NO!* Nicky Cruz had to be first and last. The one and only. The master, served meekly by the strong, feared by the weak, worshiped by the sniveling.

After he had finished preaching, someone pointed me out to him and laughed, "If you can reach Nicky, you can reach anyone."

THE SKINNY WITCH WALKED UP TO ME, looked me straight in the eyes and said, "Nicky, Jesus loves you." I couldn't believe what I heard.

My only defense was to start swearing at him and get out of there — quickly. He truly was a witch, I could tell. Within him was a supernatural authority greater than anything I'd ever felt. I had seen his kind before. He was just like my father.

As I retreated, I hoped not a soul detected how immensely threatened I felt in the presence of a man whose words and actions cowed me beyond belief. But I was not going to be intimidated.

I mocked him aloud as I strutted away. Although I kept up my swaggering bravado act as I escaped, I still felt trapped. In front of me was the snickering crowd. Behind me was this smiling, skinny witch talking about *love*. *Nobody loved me.*

Nobody ever had. As I pushed through the mob, I remembered my mother's denunciations, *"I don't love you, Nicky. You're not my son. You're the son of Satan."*

Wilkerson called to me again. I didn't know how to deal with it. "You come near me, preacher, and I'll kill you," I spat over my shoulder. My girlfriend, Lydia, and I headed up St. Edward Street. In the crowded basement room where the Mau Maus hung out, I turned the record player on as loud as it would play and began to dance with her.

But, why couldn't I drown out the sound of those four words: *"Nicky, Jesus loves you"*?

I HEARD A NOISE AT THE DOOR. Looking up, I saw the witch had followed me. He was waving his Bible and preaching. In our filthy basement, he looked ridiculous.

But I understood his witchcraft. He was intimidating me — attacking like a boxer, unafraid, secure in his supernatural superiority. "Where's Nicky?" he asked.

Nodding his head toward me, Israel quickly walked away from him. Wilkerson strolled across the room like he owned the place. With a big smile on his face, he stuck out his hand and said, "Nicky, I just wanted to shake hands with …"

Before he could finish, I slapped him in the face. Then, I spit on him.

"Nicky, they spit on Jesus, too," he said calmly as the saliva dripped off of his chin and onto his skinny tie.

I cursed him — loudly. I wanted him *gone!*

"Nicky, I just want to tell you again, *Jesus loves you.*"

I began screaming at him. In a frenzy, I knocked him down. Standing over him, I cursed his God, his mother, his Jesus and anyone I could think of that might mean something to him.

HE PULLED HIMSELF UP and with no apparent malice said, "Nicky, Jesus loves you. And so do I."

I was furious.

"Get out, you crazy witch!" I screamed at the top of my lungs. "I give you 24 hours to get off my turf or *I'll kill you!*"

Backing out the door, still smiling, he calmly repeated, "Remember, Nicky, Jesus loves you."

Didn't this lunatic know that if he pushed me any farther, I really would see him dead? Livid with anger, I picked up an empty wine bottle and smashed it to the floor. He smiled and stepped out the door.

I screamed my anger. I had never felt so frustrated, so desperate, so completely helpless in my life. The other guys could see this Wilkerson had really gotten under my skin. So, calmly, I pulled myself together.

"He is a crazy witch," I announced. "I know his kind. If he comes back, I'll set him on fire."

But I was scared. *Sleep wouldn't come that night.* I kept hearing his voice saying over and over, "Jesus loves you, Nicky. Jesus loves you, Nicky …"

I recognized that a spiritual battle was underway. But I tried to put it out of my mind. I hated everything my dad had been and done. Now, I just wanted to close my eyes to this unwelcome attack. *I didn't know how to fight back.* I hadn't paid that much attention to what Papa did. Plus I didn't want to be like him. No way.

THE ONLY PLACE WILKERSON COULD FIND to stay that night was in a nearby church. Within him, serious spiritual warfare was underway, as well.

He was filled with horrible self-doubt — *nurtured and exaggerated by Satan,* who wanted him to give up in embarrassing failure and defeat.

Wilkerson saw that he was just a country preacher. Why had he come to New York expecting to win souls, transform lives and set the world on fire for Jesus? He wasn't equipped for that! God hadn't blessed it, either. Instead, Dave had run into me.

As he knelt before the Lord, he wept, deeply stung from my repeated humiliations of him in front of everybody. Yes, seemingly through the power of the Holy Spirit, he had hung on, determined to win me to Jesus. But it looked truly hopeless. The other gang members were not impressed with his bulldog tenacity. Instead everyone on the street was laughing at this crazy man who Nicky Cruz was on the verge of strangling.

IN FERVENT PRAYER, he asked God to send him back to his family and his little church in Pennsylvania. He trembled in his growing self-doubt, wondering how he could have been so mistaken about this half-cocked mission to the inner city. Had he just embarrassed the Lord instead of lifting Him up?

He began to believe he had missed God's direction altogether. Yes, he had *felt* sure of God's direction that he go preach to the street gangs of New York City. But now...

Had it been his own ego that he had heard — and not the Lord? Had he mistaken the voice of God for his own delusions of grandeur? After all, it made no sense for a country boy to take on the task of evangelizing New York's murdering street kids.

WAITING FOR AN ANSWER, he pleaded for a sign, begging to hear the voice of the Lord. And as the night grew dark, he felt God's gentle reassurance.

Yes, he had been obedient. Yes, there would be great spiritual reward. As Wilkerson prayed, he felt increasingly burdened for this kid who had so captivated his attention: swaggering, insulting Nicky Cruz.

"Lord, give me the words," he prayed. "Fill me with your power. Change that boy's heart. He hurts so *deeply*. He's headed straight to hell. Ease his enormous pain, O Lord."

Filled with new energy, Wilkerson fell on his face and interceded into the long night for me — and got little sleep.

Nor did I. Wilkerson's prayers were sending angelic battle forces into action. A celestial rumble was underway for my soul. As he prayed, I tossed and turned and stared at the ceiling. I smoked one cigarette after another. I couldn't rest. I couldn't sleep. I did everything to silence that voice, but the words echoed in my brain throughout the night: *Nicky, Jesus loves you. Nicky, Jesus loves you."*

Finally, I turned on the light and looked at my watch — 5 A.M. No use wrestling with the pillow any longer. I got up, dressed, picked up my cigarettes, walked down the three flights of stairs and opened the front door of the decaying tenement.

The sky was just beginning to turn gray.

In the distance, I could hear the sounds of New York City as it awakened to another day. I plopped down on the front steps with my head in my hands. Still, my mind replayed the haunting refrain:

"Nicky, Jesus loves you. Nicky, Jesus loves you ..."

9

"NICKY, JESUS LOVES YOU!"

A car pulled up.

A door slammed. I lifted my weary head and focused my bloodshot eyes. The skinny Pennsylvania preacher was standing in front of me again.

How did he know where to find me? I was flabbergasted.

"Hi, Nicky!" he greeted, his voice full of joy and love and happiness. "Remember what I told you last night? I just wanted to come by and tell you once more that *Jesus loves you*."

I'd had **enough**. Leaping up, I pulled my knife.

He lurched back as I flashed the switchblade. We stood eye-to-eye — me ready to spill his blood into the filthy gutter.

But he just smiled. "You could kill me, Nicky," he whispered, his voice low and gravely. "You could cut me in a thousand pieces and lay them out on the street. But every piece would cry out, *'Nicky, Jesus loves you!'"*

Livid, I stared my hate at him. I sliced the air wickedly with my knife.

"You're deeply afraid, aren't you, Nicky?" he said, his voice gentle. "You're sick of your life. You're lonely." He spoke with great inner strength and conviction. "Jesus still loves you, Nicky."

I screamed my utter rage.

Smiling, he turned to go. I sat down on the steps and refused to even watch his car disappear down the street.

Crazy witch. Why couldn't he leave me alone? He was worse than my dad. Why couldn't everybody *LEAVE ME ALONE?*

WILKERSON DEVOTED HIMSELF to constant prayer for me. The burden of my torment built in him, night and day. He saw my gnawing hurt. He felt Jesus' love for me. Yet, everyone Dave met tried to discourage him from wasting his time on me. "Nicky's the worst. He'll never change. You're wasting your time."

Yet, God nurtured an incredible love for me in Dave's heart. Even though he was intimidated by the circumstances, he continued to pray — four hours daily. From 2 A.M. until 6 A.M., he poured out his heart and asked God to perform a miracle in my life.

Dave says he knew how close I was to killing him on several occasions over the next few days. But he simply could not give up and go away.

I grew sick to my stomach with his clever words and his big, blinking, innocent eyes. He looked like a calf, staring at me so trustingly — unconcerned that in a second I could have a blade to his jugular and his life running out into the gutter.

I grew threatened by the friendship he developed with Israel — and several others in our gang. I grew solidly convinced Wilkerson was a witch — like my dad. I began to believe Dave was up to something that none of us saw. He wanted to take over the streets. He wanted our turf.

Why? I had no idea.

When Israel announced he was turning his life over to Jesus — and that all of us should, too — I knew it was time to waste this Pennsylvania preacher ... end his stinking interruption of our lives — *forever*.

He would have to die.

Three of my Mau Maus, Hector, Willie and Albert, and I went up to my room and smoked some marijuana. We guzzled some cheap wine, too. We probably downed several beers. One of the guys might have skin-popped some heroin — I don't remember.

But we were high. And we were in the mood for death and murder. We all were sick of Wilkerson. We wanted his holy blood drying on the deadly switchblades we carried.

Hector twirled his sawed-off shotgun like some kind of baton. "You see this, Nicky? I wanna blow him *away.*"

Willie laughed. "Nicky, that guy is out to destroy the gang. He's already got Israel thinking dangerous things."

I nodded. The sweet smell of marijuana fogged the air. Willie jumped up. "Nicky," he exclaimed, "It's time we go after him."

He was right, but the marijuana had mellowed me. I wanted to be talked into Wilkerson's murder.

"What are you talking about, man?" I drawled, laid-back and stoned. "You're saying you want to kill this guy, knowing the police will be after us. Well, you've forgotten one thing! *Israel!*"

"Forget Israel." Hector said.

"DON'T YOU EVER SAY 'FORGET ISRAEL'," I bellered. "This is a family. That's our strength, and we're brothers no matter what we do. I hate that witch more than any of you. But you guys are stupid. If we blow him away and throw him in the Hudson River or in the subway, Israel'll be questioned. He'll have to talk to save himself — but I know him. He won't talk. He'll go down before he'd turn us in."

Hector was not going to give up. "Let's tell Israel about our plan. Then we'll toss a coin, and the one who calls it can blow the man away."

I walked over to the refrigerator and pulled out a beer. I pondered the problem Wilkerson's friendship with Israel presented. Israel was my best friend. I would not betray him.

Hector became furious, almost hysterical in his desire for Wilkerson's blood. I spun and grabbed his shotgun.

"You want to challenge someone?" I snarled.

"OK, OK, OK, Nicky!" he muttered. But the matter wasn't closed. We all knew Wilkerson had to die. It was just a matter of how to do it without hurting Israel.

I decided to see Israel alone the next day and talk some sense into him.

BUT WHEN I FOUND ISRAEL, he was with Wilkerson. "Hey, Nicky," Israel called, waving me across the street to where he and Dave stood talking. "How about going with me to a meeting tomorrow night?"

"I don't wanna go," I said, staring my hatred at Wilkerson. I recognized his unearthly threat. His strange strength was strong. I was powerless against this weird magic — *love.*

"Nicky, you're a chicken," sang Israel, sensing my fright. "That's it! **You're afraid to go."**

"C'mon, Israel," I muttered. "Cut it out!"

"Nicky's a chicken! Nicky's a chicken!" Israel's sing-song cut deep into my pride. He cupped his hands around his mouth and began to call out to the whole neighborhood. "Nicky's a chicken! Hey, Nicky's a chicken." Everyone could hear.

I burned with embarrassment. "Hey! Israel, you know I'm no chicken. You know I am not afraid of nobody. *Leave me alone, Israel, OK?*"

"Aw, come on Nicky, why won't you come?"

"I'm just not going to."

"Because you're chicken. You're afraid of this preacher guy. It's the first time I've ever seen you afraid."

I glared at Israel — possibly the only person in the world who could say such words to me. I glanced at Dave, who was grinning innocently. The man was dead already, I swore.

I didn't know what kind of enchantment he was working on us. But my .32-caliber revolver would bring it to a quick end. *He would not get away with this.*

Wilkerson *practiced* love. And humility. *And self-sacrifice.*

I had never seen anything like it in action — although my soul had longed to know and receive such compassion. *Now, it scared me.*

I sensed its mighty power.

Although I did not know anything about the Holy Spirit, I knew Wilkerson had enormous forces working for him. I had no idea that the work Wilkerson was accomplishing was just Almighty God's answer to his fervent prayer, manifested in boldness under the anointing of the Holy Spirit.

Anything even slightly related to the supernatural shook my confidence. I tried to quit thinking about it. But I knew this preacher was penetrating the Mau Maus as no one had ever before. The cops had tried. Drug agents had, too. Rival gangs had even attempted to plant infiltrators and spies — to break us up.

They all failed. But this witch was winning. My best friend, Israel, was listening to Dave and telling the guys that things could be different, that they could really change.

Although I fought what he was saying, a deep yearning was awakened within me. A tiny wisp of wondering rose within my evil heart. Words cannot express the feeling. But a faint question mark hung within my heart.

I WAS WILLING, SECRETLY, TO CONSIDER that maybe this guy had some answers. Outwardly I continued to denounce him and verbally abuse him. I continued to proclaim that I hated and despised his guts. And I did. But I was mystified by him. I feared him.

I wanted him dead — and out of my life and out of Israel's life. Well, as you might guess, especially if you've read my book *Run, Baby Run* or Wilkerson's book *The Cross and the Switchblade* — or seen the movie made from it — I didn't kill Wilkerson.

I brought a third of the gang to his meeting — 75 vicious Mau Maus and their girlfriends. There we proceeded to whoop it up and try to disrupt everything. We leered at the young lady singer until she cried and stumbled off stage. Then, Wilkerson asked for volunteers to take up the collection. *HA!* I was on my feet in an instant, picking out five Mau Maus.

He let us take up the offering. When it was time to take it up to him, my friends were all grinning at me — knowing that now we would split with the loot. But something incredible had happened inside me. I couldn't do it. As everyone gawked, I turned the money over to the preacher and returned to my seat. Already, I was changing.

DURING THE ALTAR CALL, I felt crushed by my sins — and conviction that Wilkerson's words about Jesus and God's love and redemption and all that were true.

What proved it to me? The man I had sworn to kill refused to stop loving me. David Wilkerson's love changed me forever. Without it, I would never have believed Jesus' love. That first night out on the street corner, if he'd preached condemnation to me, I might have really killed him — just to show him who was boss: *"So, I'm going to hell, Preacher? Guess what? I know that! Here's something for you, Preacher. You're going to beat me there!"*

And I would have squeezed the trigger over and over and over — and laughed. And wiped his blood on my friends' faces. And kicked his dead body into the filthy gutter. But with Israel at my side, I stepped forward. As Wilkerson prayed over me, he told God that I was very, very lonely.

I LOOKED UP, NOT UNDERSTANDING how Dave knew. And I saw Wilkerson was weeping, his lips trembling. He was in the presence of Jesus Christ, his friend and savior. I stared at this man, and I was touched deep in my soul. The Holy Spirit used Dave's words as he prayed for me, "God, you placed Nicky in the womb of his mother and you love him."

Then, I began crying in repentance. I was on my knees, torn apart and broken. I began to feel God's love and understand the tenderness of the One who gives life.

For the first time, I discovered something that absolutely overpowered me: two kinds of love — human and divine. When the two came together, something supernatural and heavenly happened to me, just a lowly human being. It was powerful! *Jesus loved me! And so did this preacher!* He really did! My eyes swam with tears and my chest burned with a pain so intense that I could only call out the name of "Jesus!"

IT WAS AS IF I WERE in a heavenly operating room. My cold, hurting heart for so many years had been filled with such hatred and spite. The demonic forces in my mother's life had done an insidious work in me — turning a tender eight-year-old's heart to stone and sending a stunned little boy on a hellish journey into the darkness of men's souls.

But now the Master Surgeon, Jesus Christ opened up my chest. He took out my dark, aching heart. He saw my enormous pain. And in His mighty power, he held my heart in His powerful hands. Then He kissed it. And He took the pain away. Gently he put my heart back, closed up my chest. And I knew everything was going to be OK.

I was born again.

Delivered! Released!

I was *delirious* with this feeling of divine love. No, I had not been wrong as a mistreated little boy — I was *supposed* to love people and *care* and be sensitive. I was never supposed to be on my own emotionally — me battling the whole world! No! *I was loved!* Greatly loved — by the Almighty Creator of the Universe!

AND THAT NIGHT, I sensed for the first time in my life that I was safe. Safe in the arms of Jesus. The Holy Spirit had been working me over like a boxer — using Wilkerson to pound my soul with conviction.

I dropped to my knees before my mighty Creator. The floodgates of my soul burst open. Springs of love and emotion that had nearly dried up, burst into life.

My conflict and loneliness and guilt were replaced with the most incredible sense of peace and forgiveness and bubbling, irrepressible joy.

Again I was my Papa's Little Bird, but instead of cowering in terror, now I soared high above the earth — filled with the overwhelming joy of my freedom. I had found the truth and it had set me free! Nicky Cruz was *born all over again* into a completely new creature!

And Satan was furious!

10

THE SPIRITUAL BATTLE BEGINS

I wish I could say

that when I accepted Christ, became a Christian and was filled with God's Holy Spirit, everything was sunshine and joy for the rest of my life.

It just isn't so.

Since I found God, I have had many, many wonderful times with Him. I have also had some experiences when the devil drew so close, I shudder to remember it.

Right after I accepted the Lord, all my old enemies assumed that while I was going through this insane phase of acting like a goody-goody — *going around with Wilkerson and giving my testimony at local churches and so forth* — that I was a sitting duck. It was widely known that I no longer carried a gun or my switchblade.

AFTER ALL, 25 MAU MAUS — LED BY ME — had marched down to the police precinct station and dumped our weapons onto the booking desk.

"What's going on here?" had demanded the frightened sergeant — fearing a trick. Gangs had taken over police stations before, killing officers and setting the place on fire.

We laughed. We told him what had happened the night before. We told him about Wilkerson. And we told him and the other gawking officers about Jesus. As you can imagine, the incident created quite a stir — particularly after we asked the policemen to autograph our Bibles.

Once again, we were in the newspapers. Wilkerson became an overnight sensation. He had broken through where nobody had succeeded. The notorious Mau Maus and Bishops and Phantom Lords were lugging around Bibles and preaching salvation on the street corners!

Still, quite a few old enemies hated my guts. You have to remember that gang violence is built on deep blood lust, but also on unquenchable revenge. One gang set fire to one gang president's house, so that gang kidnaps five of the first gang's girls and has a wild orgy with them in an abandoned building, slicing up their faces before releasing them.

THEN PEOPLE START GETTING KILLED. Serious war breaks out. Rumbles. Ambushes. Bodies pile up in the street. The cops come in and try to shut everything down and figure out what's going on. But even as things cool off, intense hatred grows. Close friends of the dead remember who killed their best buddy. They lie in wait for a chance to honor his memory.

So, quite a few people figured my becoming a Christian gave them a good chance to even the score with the guy they hated with such passion. After all, it was absolutely true that I no longer carried any weapons and just talked about sissy preacher stuff like peace and love and good will.

ONE OF MY OLDEST AND MOST BITTER ENEMIES was Pedro, a vicious hustler whose face I had severely disfigured in a particularly ugly fight — back when I took enormous pleasure in permanently hurting people. His hatred against me festered every time he saw his horribly scarred nose, lips and cheeks in the mirror.

When he saw the stories in the newspaper about me and my friends and Wilkerson, he saw his chance to even the score — *forever*.

He began stalking me. The first Sunday night after my conversion, he jumped me outside of church. I'd really enjoyed the worship and the sermon. I'd brought 75 of my most cold-hearted friends into the biggest service that little church had ever had.

I WAS EXCITED ABOUT JESUS and about how so many of my friends had come to know Him during the service. Well, suddenly, out of the darkness, Pedro came from nowhere, slamming a blade at my heart without warning, throwing me backward as he lunged again and again and again.

Instinctively, I shielded myself with the only thing I held — my Bible. As Pedro repeatedly stabbed the blade at my chest and throat, he instead hit my Bible. I can honestly tell you that the Word of God saved me that night — although my hands were jabbed deeply over and over.

As girls shrieked and blood went everywhere, I grabbed an automobile antenna — instinctively intending to blind Pedro with it, then finish him off with his own knife. But then, the truth hit me. *I was a new person.* I could not kill him. Things were different, now.

SUDDENLY, I UNDERSTOOD WHY PEDRO HATED ME. *I sympathized completely.* I had done a truly terrible thing to him! So, I began talking to the Lord out loud. I dropped the antenna and exclaimed, "Lord God, I ask you to protect me. Help me, Jesus. I never expected to have to ask you something like this, but take care of me. I'm not going to fight this guy."

Pedro paused. "What did you say?" he asked.

"I asked the Lord Jesus Christ to protect me," I answered. "And He will. He loves you, too, you know."

Well, Pedro began cursing me and telling me that he was going to kill me right there and prove to everybody that I was never the tough guy everybody thought I was.

I knew he meant it. "OK," I said. "Go ahead. Try to kill me. Jesus will protect me. He loves you and so do I."

He stopped. "Do you really believe all that?" he demanded.

"Yes, I do," I answered. "Jesus will protect me. I don't have to fight anybody anymore."

He stared at me — his hatred deep. And then he slipped away into the night. He easily could have killed me. But he didn't. As I walked back to the church, my deep hand wounds bleeding all over my clothes, the girls with me screamed for somebody to call an ambulance. I was rushed to the hospital where I had to undergo emergency surgery on my hand.

Imagine my confusion and turmoil as I lay in the hospital bed that night. I wondered if I had been a coward not to fight back. But, I could not deny that when I had called on the Lord to protect me, the attack had stopped. Pedro had turned and actually fled into the darkness.

SEVENTEEN YEARS PASSED before I saw him again. I went off to Bible college in California. Dave's book, *The Cross and the Switchblade,* then my own *Run, Baby, Run,* became runaway bestsellers — to everybody's surprise. Both he and I became big celebrities.

People acted like we were superstars or apostles or something. They couldn't believe he really was just a country preacher who had obeyed God — or that I was just a throwaway kid on the streets who had hardly learned to speak English.

They wanted us to be mighty men of God. The Lord was merciful, giving us the anointing to do His work when it was needed. Thousands upon thousands came to know Jesus — and still do when they hear either one of us. Why? Because Almighty God in His pleasure uses a simple thing like the story of a murderous kid and a Pennsylvania pastor to show unbelievers the glorious wonder of the Gospel.

AT A BIG CRUSADE in Chicago, I was the featured guest and had just been interviewed by the *Chicago Tribune*. The auditorium was packed with maybe 3,500 people. Another 2,700 had been put in an adjacent ballroom, listening over loudspeakers.

It's hard to explain what happened during that message. I felt their deep hurt and pain and sorrow. I knew their enormous sinfulness and their their need for repentance and forgiveness. As I made the altar call, I broke down in tears and had to apologize. I said that I knew very strongly there were people who really needed this Jesus that I was talking about — and that I loved them. More than 800 knelt around the sides of the stage. I was leading them in prayer when I saw Pedro.

He looked more rugged than before. His face was still horribly scarred, but he had grown a beard. I knew he was running from the law, too. And so, my sworn blood enemy, now a dangerous fugitive and fleeing felon — who had attempted to kill me — was pushing toward the microphone, not praying at all. He was staring at me — deadly serious. "Oh, God," I prayed silently. "Let there be no sorrow here after we have had such *joy.*"

I BEGAN TO WALK TOWARD PEDRO, deciding I would try to grab him in a bear-hug — pinning his hands down while those around me, *hopefully,* figured out what was happening.

"Nicky," he said, staring at me. "Nicky."

"Pedro," I answered solemnly, trying to see if he already had a gun or maybe a knife in his hand.

"I want Jesus," he said. There were tears in his eyes. "You've touched me. You've really touched my heart. I came here to kill you. I sat up there on the second balcony planning to blow you away. But you and these people have touched me. I want that Jesus. I want him now."

My fear turned to joy. We embraced, excitedly. But, I could feel the gun under his coat. We knelt together, crying, hugging. We forgave each other with deep thanks and sorrow and respect.

He received Jesus into his heart.

But Satan would try again.

And again.

11

HORRIBLE EVIL IN OUR BEDROOM

Shortly after I married Gloria,
the beautiful girl of my dreams, I was holding a youth crusade in a southern city. My bride and I stayed in a rooming house owned by a Reverend Smith. He was pastor of a large church and had quite a reputation for his work with children and young people. He was always having conferences and camps and retreats for kids, and seemed like a pleasant enough man.

Certainly he was a successful, hard-working minister. But there was something immensely evil about him that repelled me. I certainly was not prepared to denounce him. I had no evidence. Just a very bad feeling.

And something about the house smelled of evil. I couldn't put my finger on it at the time, although I sensed something wrong. Many of us felt it. When we gathered in the prayer room, there was a note of special urgency in the petitions. "Deliver us from evil" became our constant request.

I had some great times working with his outreach's young people and winning many of them to the Lord. *It was heady work. The kids were hungry for Jesus*. How could this be? They went to a reputable church!

The dilemma drove me to my knees, into the Bible and into long hours of prayer and times of fasting.

IN THE MIDST OF MY SEARCH CAME AN EXPERIENCE that is still horrible for me to remember. One night there in that preacher's boarding house, as Gloria slept, I tossed and turned.

The sense of evil was *there* in the house. You may not believe that evil can permeate a specific place or person, but I have experienced it many times. I have seen many drug addicts that I know are possessed by Satan. I know when the devil walks into a room.

That night I felt him in mine.

GLORIA TURNED IN HER SLEEP and the street light fell across her lovely throat. A murderous impulse came into my mind. *Choke her, it urged.*

The thought was so contrary to anything I could imagine, I was appalled. I jumped out of bed, fled to the room next to ours and dropped to my knees beside an empty cot. Fear chilled my stomach. I felt as weak as a baby.

"Lord," I cried out, "help me! You know how I love Gloria. Help me get rid of this awful thought. Help me!"

A horrible command flashed across my consciousness again. *Kill Gloria.*

"No!" I almost shrieked. "Jesus — where are You?"

I wondered if I was going insane. I felt so weak I held on to the mattress. The room circled around me. *What was happening?*

A SPIRIT OF DESTRUCTION HUNG LIKE A HEAVY FOG in the air. In another room, a co-worker Larry White, bolted awake, feeling the same sense of impending destruction, of an evil, murderous attack. He jumped out of his bed and began to pray.

I went back to my room. As I stood over Gloria, something slimy and indecent said, *Choke her.*

"Wake up!" I cried as I grabbed her hand. "Wake up! I need you! "

"I'm tired, sweetheart," moaned Gloria, as she started to turn over.

"No, Gloria! Wake up! Something is wrong. I'm losing my mind, pray for me!" I shook her urgently. "Gloria you've got to help me. *The devil is here.* Get up — please — and help me fight back."

Gloria came awake and reached for the Bible. "Let me read you a Psalm," she said. This was one time I didn't want the Bible read.

"There's no time for that, Gloria. Don't do anything right now but pray! Somebody wants to destroy us. Pray!"

I PRAYED ALOUD AS SHE KNELT WITH ME. I reminded God of His promises to defend us against evil. I told Him there was only one thing I wanted, to love and serve Him, but I needed His help — and I needed it *NOW!* I pleaded with Him to help me overcome the power of Satan. Then

Gloria prayed. She didn't say as much as I did, but as she talked to Jesus, I felt His power beginning to cover me like a shield.

"Gloria," I said, "I've just had a terrible temptation. It's too awful to even tell you about now. Lay your hands on me, Gloria, and plead the blood of Jesus against the devil."

Gloria laid her cool, firm hands on my head and offered the most wonderful prayer. I felt the strength of the Holy Spirit flow into me. When she had finished, I knew that the tempter had gone.

When we got back into bed, Gloria pressed my hand. "What happened, Nicky?" she asked.

I told her.

I told her the whole impossible story as truthfully and completely as I knew how. You can get an idea of what a great Christian and great person Gloria is when I say that she has never let that experience make the slightest rift between us.

But what brought such evil into our room?

Still shaken, I told Gloria to go back to sleep while I went to the prayer room to pray some more. I found five other workers already there with Larry White. They all had felt the evil presence and were seeking the only defense there is. "Jesus," I implored, "kick the devil out of here!"

WE SAID IT MANY DIFFERENT WAYS, but that was the thing we all asked for. And God answered. The spirit of oppression lifted and we went back the next day to snatching souls from the Evil One.

I have thought about the incident many times. If I had told a psychiatrist about it, I have no doubt that he would have labeled me a murderous psychotic.

I'm no psychiatrist, but I know just enough about such things to realize that I had been in a very dangerous condition.

Was my mind going?

Was the power of Satan too much for me?

Why had I let those murderous impulses into my mind?

Why Gloria — of all people? God knows how much she means to me. He picked her out of all the girls on earth just for me, and many is the time she and her influence have kept me from wrong.

What had brought such horrible evil into our room?

12

DON'T GIVE SATAN AUTHORITY IN YOUR LIFE!

As the crusade continued,

hundreds of kids came to Jesus. It was a glorious time of great victory. But, then in the next days, some parents in Rev. Smith's church came to me with some very serious questions about secret sins their little boys had begun admitting.

I was stunned. But the confessions rang too true to ignore. Listening to the sobbing testimony of these tender little Christians our crusade had led to Jesus, I knew the source of the terrible evil in my room that night. I had been right about Rev. Smith being dreadfully evil — although I had been too naive to act immediately on it.

He was a longtime sexual abuser of children.

For years he had been molesting the youth of his church — youngsters the Lord had saved now in our services.

I was enraged.

Anyone who does such a terrible thing — *knowing how plainly the Bible talks about what will happen to someone who causes a little one to quit believing in Jesus*—must belong to Satan. The reports led to an official inquiry.

After an investigation, formal charges were filled.

ON THE TESTIMONY OF THE BOYS and of doctors who examined them, Rev. Smith was defrocked — removed from the ministry — for homosexual molestation.

What am I telling you? That Satan possesses homosexuals? Not necessarily. But when we men or women of God open ourselves up to evil — by practicing even one secret sin — the devil loves it!

He comes in with all his evil might!

When you open the door, he comes slamming in with all his death and destruction. After all, what a marvelous opportunity to destroy the work of Jesus Christ! Just look what can happen if Satan can get a pastor — whom new, tender Christians trust and on whom mature Christians depend — to betray his flock!

And just look at all the nasty publicity when that pastor is unmasked before the sneering, finger-pointing world! How many hundreds will stumble in their walk with Jesus? How many doubters will hoot their derision — and harden their hearts totally to the Gospel?

BUT IT IS MORE THAN THAT. I've already shared with you about fortifying your mind and spirit with the Word of God.

That's an incredibly effective tactic that you must put to work in your battle with the devil. But here is another that you cannot ignore.

You cannot practice secret sin. You cannot hold onto one little, favorite evil — and give everything else to Jesus. Satan will use that one little foothold to do all he can to destroy you.

You must do everything possible not to allow Satan to have any authority over any part of your life. Oh, Nicky, you may say, that sounds easy. Do I mean that you need to declare that Satan has no business messing around with you?

Sure! Say it! Declare it! Let him know where you stand.

But here's where an old saying has enormous spiritual truth: *"Actions speak louder than words."*

YOU CAN MARCH AROUND DECLARING that Satan has no place in your life — but if your actions give him a secret place in your heart, all your proclamations will do little good!

What actions should you take? According to Romans 8:3, "We aren't saved from sin's grasp by knowing the commandments of God, because we can't and don't keep them ..."

So, we can't be good by ourselves. Then, how are we supposed to be good?

A short epistle in the very back of the New Testament, 1 John, is a marvelous road map for the Christian trying to live without sin. Start with 1 John 1:5-7: "This is the message God has given us to pass on to you: that God is Light and in him is no darkness at all. So if we say we are his friends, but go on living in spiritual darkness and sin, we are lying. But if we are living in the light of God's presence, just as Christ does, then we have wonderful fellowship and joy with each other, and the blood of Jesus his Son cleanses us from every sin."

That doesn't say anything about trying to keep all the rules, does it?

IT SAYS WE ARE TO ENJOY FELLOWSHIP with God! But don't we have to be *really* pure and holy for God to want to fellowship with us? NO! Not at all! Keep reading verses 8 and 9: "If we say that we have no sin, we are only fooling ourselves, and refusing to accept the truth. But if we confess our sins to him, he can be depended on to forgive us and to cleanse us from every wrong."

Do you get that? Imperfect, we can fellowship with God anyway, admitting to him our failures — and he just wipes the slate clean! We don't have to live in guilt and shame or even come up with game plans and rule books to help us be holy. We're just supposed to get to know our Father — and talk to Him frankly about our sins, temptations, imperfections, failures and weaknesses.

Then, as a result of these godly chats, are we supposed to emerge completely perfect? Keep reading 1 John, moving into the second chapter. Pause on verses 1 and 12: "My little children, I am telling you this so that you will stay away from sin. But if you sin, there is someone to plead for you before the Father. His name is Jesus Christ, the one who is all that is good and who pleases God completely. I am writing these things to all of you, my little children, because your sins have been forgiven in the name of Jesus our Savior."

What a relief! God knows that even Christians sin!
What marvelous hope!

WE AREN'T EXPECTED TO BE PERFECT! I don't know about you, but I consider that incredible news! But, Nicky, you might protest, what are we supposed to do, if we're not expected to keep track of all the rules? Let's continue reading in the second chapter of 1 John. Pause on verse 28:

"And now, my little children, stay in happy fellowship with the Lord so that when he comes, you will not have to be ashamed and shrink back from meeting him."

Think about that. The repeated instruction we're given is that we're supposed to "stay in happy fellowship" with the Lord! Our mighty, loving Creator invites us to grow ever closer and closer to Him daily. Why? Well, one reason is that when we obey, we constantly become Christ-like as we mature! Look at Romans 8:6: "Following after the Holy Spirit leads to life and peace ..."

What's the alternative? Terrible punishment?

Yes, but it's the self-imposed sort. We do it to ourselves. The verse continues: "... but following after the old nature leads to death." The old *King James Version* says the same thing: "For to be carnally minded is death; but to be spiritually minded is life and peace."

What happens is that as we become more and more like Christ, we just don't want to sin. We're not "carnally minded" anymore. *Carnally minded?*

That happens when we don't fellowship with God, don't become Christ-like and continue living in normal human selfishness and self-centeredness. To be carnally minded is to live the *American pleasure principle*, giving in to our hungers and lusts and ambitions — caring more about yourself than about Jesus. Loving yourself more than your fellow man. Growing ever more selfish. Ugly. Wicked. Evil.

Can a Christian be "carnally minded?" If your desire is not to know God, you will seek fulfillment in the sensations of pleasure. All you will care about is yourself and feeling good. Satisfying your urges will become more important to you than being Christ-like.

You'll rationalize away your conscience.

Even though you may keep wearing what the world sees as the spiritual uniform of a Christian, you'll become increasingly carnal, doing whatever is necessary to give yourself a thrill.

Like the Rev. Smith did. And look at the terrible damage that resulted! Not only did Rev. Smith sink into degradation and separation from his loving Creator, he began taking innocent, trusting kids with him. *Look how Satan used him!*

BUT YOU DON'T HAVE TO BE A CHILD-MOLESTER to sink into carnal mindedness, my friend. You can merely be selfish.

This is one of my greatest heartaches as I look out at church auditoriums. So many church members are not becoming more Christlike — but are just getting more and more selfish!

Are you a selfish, carnal Christian? Instead of spending an hour with the Lord at the start of the day, would you rather do *anything* else? Do you have all your excuses lined up and ready? The day has to start early since you have such a heavy workload. You're too exhausted to get up early and pray. The responsibility of getting the kids to school and the spouse off to work just make it impossible for you to have a quiet time with God?

Instead of having a servant's heart, do you sit in church demanding to be blessed, entertained and assured you're OK — and God loves you?

Do you ignore His urgent call to feed his lambs or rescue the perishing? Instead, do you sit in your seat like a big Christian sheep, demanding to be fed: *BAA! BAA! BAA! Feed me! Make me feel good about myself!*

Your church needs workers in the nursery? *BAA! I don't feel called!* The mission field needs Bible translators? *BAA! I'm not qualified nor interested in getting qualified.*

The street witnessing team needs Christian homes to take in the homeless? The pregnancy counseling hotline needs volunteers from midnight to 6 a.m.? The drug abuse center needs believers to spend time with suicidal teens? *BAA! BAA! BAA! Not me! I don't hear the call. Feed me! Feed me! I want to feel good about myself!*

WHEN YOU HAVE SELFISH SIN IN YOUR LIFE, there is no strength, my friend! You are going to have a terrible time battling Satan!

If we go back and look at some of the harsh warnings in 1 John, you'll see selfish Christians really have something to worry about. Look at 1 John 3:10, 16-18: "So now we can tell who is a child of God and who belongs to Satan. Whoever is living a life of sin and doesn't love his brother shows he is not in God's family. We know what real love is from Christ's example in dying for us. And so we also ought to lay down our lives for our Christian brothers. But if someone who is supposed to be a Christian has money enough to live well, and sees a brother in need, and won't help him — how can God's love be within him? Little children, let us stop just saying we love people; let us really love them, and show it by our actions."

What's the answer? How do you get selfishness and other sin out of your life? Keep reading! In chapter 4, pause at verses 7 and 17:

"Dear friends, let us practice loving each other, for love comes from God and those who are loving and kind show that they are the children of God, and that they are getting to know him better. And as we live with Christ, our love grows more perfect and complete; so we will not be ashamed and embarrassed at the day of judgment, but can face him with confidence and joy, because he loves us and we love him too."

DID YOU GET THAT? Our love grows more perfect and complete! As a result, we don't have anything to be ashamed of! Yes!

So, do we work at being perfect or at loving one another?

We work at love. And we become righteous. What happens? Read verse 18 in the final chapter 5: "No one who has become part of God's family makes a practice of sinning, for Christ, God's son, holds him securely and the devil cannot get his hands on him."

Praise God! *We are protected!* "But, Nicky," you may be saying, "I am having real trouble living a Christian life." You're trying, but it just isn't happening. You aren't growing closer to God. And, frankly, you don't like Christians you know who you believe are hypocrites and snobs and crooks.

Pray! Ask the Father to reveal *your* sin to you! *He will!* Remember that 1John 1:9 promises us: "But if we confess our sins to him, he can be depended on to forgive us and to cleanse us from every wrong."

*Don't just **skip over that**, my friend!* I want you to be an effective spiritual warrior. I want you to be victorious over Satan. As a righteous Christian, you have authority and power!

But are you still having problems? Has the Lord perhaps not revealed to you your sin? Well, keep after Him! How? Through daily prayer. Take a daily quiet time with the Lord at dawn. You'll be astonished at its effect on your life. You're going to grow closer to God. You're going to enjoy His presence. You're going to see sin that needs to be corrected and you're going to start benefiting from all those promises in 1 John.

In summary, my friend, God has shown us a different way to heaven. It's not by "being good enough" and trying to obey each of God's rules for living. Romans 3 proclaims that "God says he will accept us and acquit us — declare us 'not guilty' — if we trust Jesus Christ to take away our sins."

BE CAREFUL NOT TO THINK OF HOLINESS as some spiritual trophy to be won or earned. Holiness cannot be attained by tithing, by good deeds, nor by intellectual knowledge. It results as we fellowship with the Lord. Although personal one-on-one quiet time in the morning is one of the most effective ways to fellowship with God, it is not the only way.

• We fellowship with Him in our worship and praise. You'll grow in your understanding of the Almighty as you participate in sincere worship.

• You grow to know the Lord when you sit under good preaching.

• When you fellowship with God's people, you begin to see Him at work in their lives and better understand His ways. Be careful not to expect fellow Christians to be Christ. None of us are. We are human, just like you.

• Bible reading is essential as you grow to know and love the Lord. He gave us a road map: the Bible. Furthermore, it will show you how God dealt with His people in the past — which is a pretty good indication of how you can expect Him to deal with His people today.

• You'll learn a great deal about the Lord when you put feet on your faith and get to work in His work. Holiness is not a passive life of sitting around being nice and sweet and good. Holiness produces a willingness to dig in and do unpleasant tasks, to care for the unlovely and the ungrateful, and to sacrifice one's personal pride and ambitions for the Kingdom. Witnessing at a rock concert will require you to depend on Him. So will teaching a five-year-old Sunday school class.

But don't expect any of this to earn holiness. Holiness is a gift from God. I've said that a number of times in this book. But let me say it again. Just as we are — sinful and imperfect, we are invited to fellowship with Him. Then, He will change us.

"...I am the Lord, who makes you holy," God instructed Moses in Exodus 31:13.

Holiness is an outgrowth of our fellowship with God. The more we fellowship with Him, the holier we become. But when you cease to fellowship with your Lord and Savior, your eyes shift off of Him and onto the lies of unsatisfying sin.

Then, quickly, you render yourself ineffective in the battlefield! You become a prisoner of war, taken captive by Satan because of festering, ulcerating, cancerous sins in your life!

Is this too hard?

Am I asking too much of you my Christian friend? Are you too imperfect to make this work?

No. Look at I John 1:9 one more time: *"If we confess our sins, he is faithful and just to forgive us our sins, and to cleanse us from all unrighteousness."*

What a marvelous promise for us Christians! The devil would like you to get bogged down in a personal obsession to achieve holiness and righteousness, discouraged because you cannot become perfect.

He'd like to distort that particular truth to frustrate you.

He wants you to believe that you cannot fight back unless you are completely without sin in your life. Well, you have a promise that if you confess your sin, you are forgiven! By God's grace, you are without sin! And furthermore, God wants to fellowship with you even if you are fighting a seemingly losing battle with sin.

He wants you to be *free!* He will help you win!

In order to do this, God wants to be your daily companion. Your friend. Your first and last line of defense. The Protector you run to at the first sign of trouble. The Provider that you know will not let your children beg for food. The Teacher who wants you to grow into righteousness. The Savior whose angels get delirious with joy when the news is announced that one more human has decided to spend eternity with them!

This mighty God with whom you fellowship on a daily, steady basis will give you a wall of fire to protect you from the devil. What is that wall? *Holiness and righteousness!* Satan can't get you because you tattle on him to Almighty God everytime that something is giving you trouble!

Don't think I dreamed this up.

A little shepherd boy who became a mighty king and whose star became the historic symbol of Isreal wrote about it constantly. Look at all the mighty promises that fill David's Psalms. Sit down and read three or four of them!

The righteous and holy are protected!

13

YOU'RE NOT A CAPTIVE OF YOUR THOUGHTS!

After the horrible attack

in which the devil urged me to murder my beloved Gloria, you can imagine the inner turmoil and doubt that I went through!

Was I a crazy man?

A schizophrenic — dangerous — needing to be locked up?

I was so blessed to have as a friend the Rev. Esteban Camarillo — who had been my teacher at Bible college. I told him about that terrible night and other times when the Evil One seemed so close — even after I had become a Christian. I left out nothing, knowing that here was a man who would understand, perhaps even help me understand those experiences.

When I had finished telling about them, I asked, "What do you think? Is there any hope for me?"

"Nicky," said this man of God with a smile, "do you think you're the only one the devil is after?"

"No, but these horrible thoughts were right in my mind! What kind of a person am I?"

"Nicky, you're the same kind of person as anyone else the devil has lost but is still trying to get back. First of all, think of where you were both times. Right on the devil's turf, as you fellows would say! You were beating the devil at his own business, snatching human beings from his grip, and he doesn't like that! So like a roaring lion he comes after you.

"AS TO THOUGHTS — MARTIN LUTHER USED TO SAY they're like birds. You can't help it if they fly over your head, but you don't need to let them build nests in your hair! Satan is a clever being, Nicky. I wish I could say there were never any evil thoughts in my mind, but I can't. One thing is for sure. When you called on God for help, you did exactly the right thing. Resist the devil and he has to flee from you. Resist him with God's help and you can't lose.

"Nicky, do you remember when Jesus was tempted? Look up the fourth chapter of Luke. Some say Satan came to Him in bodily form; some say it was a mental or spiritual temptation. Whichever it was, even He was tempted by the devil, so is it surprising that you were?"

Since that talk with the Reverend Camarillo I have never been oppressed the same way again. And I have come to realize some other things about Satan. Jesus called him a liar and a murderer in John 8:44.

Gloria is the one person on earth I love most, and is a tremendous help to me in every way. How Satan would like to destroy her — *and me at the same time!*

Another thing: Both times I was so oppressed by Satan, I realize I was overdoing the fasting. I still fast on special occasions, but I have come to realize an important secret of the Christian life. God wants us strong mentally, spiritually, and physically. When we become weak at any point, Satan tries to slip past our guard at that point. Important as fasting may sometimes be, the devil can use even that to try to get the better of us.

BUT I HAVE COME TO AN ASSURANCE ABOUT THAT. As I agonized about what had happened when I seemed to be almost back in the clutches of Satan, Jesus gave me a marvelous word of assurance. He said to me:

Nicky, there is no way the devil can have you. He will never stop trying, but so long as you trust Me, he will never be able to move you one fraction of an inch from the hollow of my hand.

When I read passages like John 10:27, 28, I realize this promise is for everyone. And I'm glad these things happened, horrible as they were to go through at the time. They have taught me how much you have to depend on Christ all the time:

Because you never know what Satan will try next!

14

SATAN WANTS THE INNOCENT, LITTLE ONES

Some years into my ministry

I flew to Chicago to hold a crusade with the help of John Ambrose, a sales executive and good friend. As I settled down for the ride to his home, I remembered the first time I had spoken in his city, and of some of the great young people who had helped make that earlier crusade successful.

"Do you remember Olga Santiri?" asked John.

I tried to place the name.

"I would be surprised if you did remember her, really. She's one of the girls in our church that never made much of an impression on anyone. But she phoned twice yesterday — says she's got to see you."

WE WERE JUST STARTING DINNER at the Ambrose home when the phone rang and the voice that came over it was very insistent. So, in spite of my travel fatigue, I agreed to see Olga that evening. John and his wife left us alone in the living room as she poured out her story.

Olga, a tall, thin girl who looked about 18, kept clasping and unclasping her hands as she talked.

"I don't know what to do," she said in a dead voice. The story that poured out of those pale lips shook me.

Olga's father had left home years before. Her mother had recently been doing some strange things. She had redecorated their basement recreation room in what Olga called a "spooky" manner, and every few weeks either her mother was away for much of the night, or "her weird friends" met in her basement.

"Weird?" I asked.

"Yes, I mean *weird!*" Olga said in a voice was beginning to get sharper and higher-pitched. "You should see the way they look, Nicky. Two of those men look like the devil himself. And the sounds and smells that fill the house when they meet in our basement!"

"OLGA," I SAID, "THAT SOUNDS A LOT like the way some parents talk to me about their children."

"But this is different," she said. "They met at our house about two weeks ago. I was baby-sitting, but I got home early and when my mother heard me come in she rushed upstairs with the funniest look on her face. 'You're a big girl now,' she said. 'Olga, and there are some things you might as well learn.'

"Mama told me to come down to the basement," Olga went on, "and there were at least a dozen people down there. It was something like a church service — only backwards, Nicky. They said the Lord's Prayer backwards. Mama had fixed up a sort of altar with black candles on it and there was a cross hung on the wall behind it — upside down!

"Nicky, they read some awful things out of a black book and they said some prayers — not to God but to spirits with weird names. I remember one prayer was to Lucifer. There was some 'spirit of ancient power' they called on to 'come up from the fiery depths' and I think he came, Nicky.

"There was a moment after that when everything was as quiet as a tomb, and then you could feel something wicked coming into the basement. There was a lot of incense burning, and I think some people were smoking pot. I'm not sure now, but the air seemed to get thicker and darker and I could see a change coming into different people's faces.

"Someone started a crazy record playing. My mother took her shoes off, different people took some of their clothes off, and one woman and two men took off everything, and they all started dancing around and around the room. Some of them started barking like dogs.

"I NOTICED ONE OF THE MEN KEPT LOOKING AT ME in a funny way — which scared me. I was a virgin, I was saving myself … and all of a sudden he grabbed my wrists and forced me to go off into a dark corner…"

Olga started to sob. It broke my heart. I prayed for words to help her.

"He hurt me, Nicky!" she sobbed. "He was like a mad dog — only worse! He forced me to have sex. Then two other men came over — *I'm so ashamed I wish I was dead!"*

"Does your mother know what happened?" I asked.

"Of course she knows! I think she's glad! I heard her on the phone talking to someone about her 'goody-goody,' and I think she believes in one of the prayers they made that night. *Evil be my good.* Nicky, I don't think those people would stop at anything."

God gave me words I never could have thought of by myself, words that brought some measure of comfort to a badly bruised little heart. We asked John and his wife to come in and join us in prayer that Olga might find again the Lord's forgiveness and joy, and His deliverance from evil.

ONE OF THE MOST HORRIBLE THINGS that Satan had done to little Olga was to deceive her into thinking that she was soiled now — impure, less than acceptable ... and damned to hell.

She sobbed as she worried aloud about sexual union with a devil-worshiper. Didn't that make them one flesh? During the rape, the satanists had chanted around her that now she was one of them — whether she liked it or not. That she was condemned and cursed to hell for all eternity.

"No, you are not," I said solemnly, looking directly into her eyes. "Olga, I have been subjected to this same sort of evil, but Jesus never blames us for things others force us to do."

She stared at me in disbelief.

"You did not sin," I told her. "You were raped. You didn't cooperate. But even if you had, it wouldn't matter. *Today, you have reaffirmed your choice to be a child of God.* Olga, you are given that *choice* by the Creator of the universe. Your salvation today is between you and Him! Nobody but Almighty God can condemn you to hell. And He has offered you complete forgiveness and absolute healing from anything that others did to you."

She nodded and sniffled. "But how can I ever be clean again?"

"You already are," I told her. "In Jesus' eyes, you are spotless and pure. You are filled with the Lord's holiness!"

HOW WONDERFUL THAT IS! Holiness is the distinctive mark and signature of God in our lives. It speaks of the way in which God separates us, calls us out to be His servants.

Holiness is not tears. Neither is it holy-sounding words we use. If you ask Him, God will strengthen you to press toward holiness in repentance and *obedience.* That's right! To get the blemish of sin out of our lives, we have to be willing to obey God. If you stick to that, you'll find yourself growing increasingly immune to the devices of the Evil One. How can even a holy person like Olga fight back?

FIRST OF ALL, SOMETIMES WE HAVE TO BE CAREFUL not to be "too heavenly minded and no earthly good."

Yes, seek the Lord in all things. But be ready to take action — to put legs on your faith. That's what James 2:17 commands. Be ready to take action to flee evil, after all I Corinthians 10:13 promises that you'll have such an escape route when evil is about to overtake you.

Do whatever is necessary not to get yourself again into such a situation where you are forced into evil. If you are under age and your parents or guardians are subjecting you to this sort of abuse, call the police. Pick up the phone and call 911. Tell the dispatcher what happened. If you have to be a bit dramatic, do it — but let the officer understand that you are very scared that it will happen again ... and that you need immediate help!

If the threat is not immediate, tell a school counselor — or your pastor. Sometimes, regrettably, people are timid about helping a child who is accusing his parents. So, tell more than one person. Spread the word that you are being subjected to horrible evil and that you need help *now!*

If you are an adult and being subjected to such evil, you may need to flee the situation, too. If laws are being broken and your kids are threatened, the police will help you. Call 911. Many towns have abuse hotlines, too.

BUT, NICKY, YOU MAY BE PROTESTING, can't you give us some spiritual advice? Can't we resist Satan — and he will flee?

Absolutely. Read I Corinthians 10:13 carefully: "But remember this — the wrong desires that come into your life aren't anything new and different. Many others have faced exactly the same problems before you. And no temptation is irresistible. You can trust God to keep the temptation from becoming so strong that you can't stand up against it, for he has promised this and will do what he says. He will show you how to escape temptation's power so that you can bear up patiently against it."

So, one way that we are told to fight back is to *get away* from things that are seemingly irresistible. *Run.* Look at Genesis 39 and you'll see that when Joseph was tempted to commit adultery with his boss's wife, he didn't try to counsel her or kneel in prayer with her.

Instead, he got out of there!
But do we always have to run?
No!

15

WE HAVE INCREDIBLE AUTHORITY!

Running isn't always

the answer. *Certainly not!* Just before Christ ascended into heaven after spending time with his followers after his Resurrection — after conquering death and Satan — he gave us some amazing authority:

"You are to go into all the world and preach the Good News to everyone, everywhere. Those who believe and are baptized will be saved. But those who refuse to believe will be condemned" (Mark 16: 15-16).

Keep reading and you will see what Jesus said we are also to do: "And those who believe shall use *my authority* to cast out demons, and they shall speak new languages. They will be able even to handle snakes with safety, and if they drink anything poisonous, it won't hurt them; and they will be able to place their hands on the sick and heal them."

What? Does that mean that you and I can do that sort of thing. *It certainly does.*

Then, why don't we?

TODAY, IT HAS BECOME VERY POPULAR for Christians who don't believe these verses to deny that any believer in Jesus still can exercise this sort of powerful authority.

Sadly, the Bible warns us against such doubters. Read 2 Timothy 3:1-5. It says, in part: "You may as well know this, too, Timothy, that in the last days it is going to be very difficult to be a Christian. For people will love only themselves and their money ... They will go to church, yes, but they won't really believe anything they hear. Don't be taken in by people like that."

The traditional *King James Version* describes these dangerous Christians as "having a form of godliness, but denying the power thereof; from such turn away."

So, be very, very careful of people who want to argue with you that there is no power in being a believer, no more healing today and no more mighty signs and wonders. Even if you have been an eyewitness to great miracles, it is amazing how persuasive these people can be! They love to cast all sorts of doubts on your faith.

Like Saul persecuting Christians before his Damascus road experiences, they are incredibly sincere — and convinced that they are doing God's work by destroying your belief in these important promises. After all, the doubters don't have any power — so, they make themselves feel less destitute by convincing you that your power is your imagination ... or from the devil!

ONE FAVORITE ARGUMENT THEY RAISE IS: "If you really have power, then why isn't everyone you pray for healed? How come you don't go out to the graveyard and raise everybody there from the dead? Why don't you walk past the hospital and heal everybody inside?"

They go on to exclaim that such absolute power was demonstrated in the New Testament — and that it was just a brief thing that faded when the Apostles — *and the ones on which they laid hands personally* — died.

BUT THERE ARE ALL SORT OF PROBLEMS with this! First, history has all sorts of records of miracles in the lives of the holy leaders of the church — even in the Dark Ages!

But our doubting friends say that such power today is *false* — *from Satan* — since everyone isn't healed. Everyone was healed in the Bible, they say. Everybody who was prayed for had a mighty miracle. *Everybody.*
Not so!

Read Mark 6:5 carefully, my friend. Get two or three translations to make sure that you understand what it says. The passage describes a time when Jesus was unable to get much accomplished in terms of his usual miracles because the people where he was did not believe.
Read it!

Then, there is Matthew 17:16-21 in which the apostles were incredibly frustrated when they failed to cast out a demon. Jesus told them that this sort of demon came out only with much prayer and fasting.

So, the fact that some are not healed today is no proof that we do not have the same power — which the Bible repeatedly assures us we do have. The writer of much of the New Testament, the Apostle Paul, was not healed of an unidentified ailment called his "thorn in the flesh." *Why?* After all, he had the power to lay hands on others. He was in constant contact with other apostles and those on whom the apostles had laid hands. *Yet, God chose not to heal him!*

Why? Because God alone is God.

HE CHOOSES WHO WILL BE HEALED. He knows in His immense wisdom and understanding what mighty work should happen here and now … and what should wait, or perhaps not occur at all!

So, rather than argue with your friends who don't believe that we Christians have any sort of authority over evil, you will be much happier and fulfilled if you just choose to believe the Bible's many promises.

We are given immense authority over the Evil One, according to Luke 10: 17-20. Read it!

John 14: 12-14 is even more clear: "In solemn truth I tell you, anyone believing in me shall do the same miracles I have done, and even greater ones, because I am going to be with the Father. You can ask him for anything, using my name, and I will do it, for this will bring praise to the Father because of what I, the Son, will do for you. Yes, ask anything, using my name and I will do it!"

Are we supposed to worry about those two passages where the apostles and even Jesus did not have the desired results? No! Jesus didn't discourage His disciples when they failed. Matthew 17:19-21 tells us:

"Afterwards the disciples asked Jesus privately, 'Why couldn't we cast that demon out?' 'Because of your little faith,' Jesus told them. 'For if you had faith even as small as a tiny mustard seed you could say to this mountain, "Move," and it would go far away. Nothing would be impossible. But this kinds of demon won't leave unless you have prayed and gone without food.'"

SO, GO BACK AND CLAIM JOHN 14: 12-14 as your very own promise. If you don't have results, fast and pray! And rest in the wonderful truth that God is in control.

And know that you have authority!

What does that mean?

He promises that whatever you request in the name of Jesus Christ, the forces of heaven go to work for you!

Remember when Daniel prayed, asking God why he'd prayed for three full weeks without getting his request? Suddenly, Daniel was given a great vision, described in Daniel 10:11-13: "And I heard his voice — 'O Daniel, greatly beloved of God,' he said, 'stand up and listen carefully to what I have to say to you, for God has sent me to you.' So, I stood up, still trembling with fear.

"Then he said, 'Don't be frightened, Daniel, for your request has been heard in heaven and was answered the very first day you began to fast before the Lord and pray for understanding; that day I was sent here to meet you. But for twenty-one days the mighty Evil Spirit who overrules the kingdom of Persia blocked my way. Then Michael, one of the top officers of the heavenly army, came to help me, so that I was able to break through these spirit rulers of Persia ..."

So, hold fast! Be patient! Remember that God does not give you a stone when you ask for bread. Remember, too, that Jesus told us in Luke 18: 2-8 to keep praying when we do not immediately get what we request!

Be bold in your faith! Fight on!

DECLARE YOUR AUTHORITY TO THE DEVIL. Let him know that you're aware of your power over him! Let him know that he is defeated! *Quote the Bible's promises* at Satan. Tell him:

"Satan, you cannot hurt me because 2 John 5:18 declares that since I belong to Jesus, you cannot even touch me!"

Or "Ephesians 1:21 tells you that God gave Jesus Christ a mighty name above every name — even over yours, Satan! So, in the mighty name of Jesus, I command you to go! Leave us alone. Take your evil demons and be gone!"

But, Nicky, you may be saying now, all that is very interesting theologically ... but is the devil really so active today? Aren't we getting a little too wrapped up in Satan's supposed activities?

Do I really swallow all these wild tales of satanists doing all these disgusting things? Is it perhaps just stuff the supermarket tabloid newspapers have made up to scare people?

No.

16

HUMAN SACRIFICE HERE AND NOW!

I did not have any trouble

believing Olga's story. Rape and perversion stories are being told worldwide by victims of satanic cults.

One of the most famous ones has to be the appalling story of a large day care center in San Francisco. There, police uncovered more than 150 cases of pre-schoolers being forced to participate in satanic ritual sex and animal mutilation.

Only as the youngsters became old enough to talk about their ordeal did the scope of the horrible case draw police attention. Lt. Larry Jones, a Boise, Idaho, law enforcement professional, says satanic assault on children is an increasing problem. He and others point to the flood of adults and teens who tell of having been ritualistically abused as children. Across the country, they are seeking counseling and deliverance, telling dreadful stories kept secret for decades.

Their descriptions are remarkably similar to the ones of the children in today's cases.

JOAN CHRISTIANSON TELLS OF BEING RAISED in a well-organized satanic cult that abused children. The California woman speaks to therapists and police officers under the sponsorship of the California Consortium of Child Abuse Councils.

She says the public needs a "basic foundation in good versus evil" to understand why some occult or satanic groups might practice ritualistic abuse. She says one of their basic strategies is to corrupt what the Bible teaches, particularly with regard to children.

"If they can destroy children's innocence without destroying their lives, they can receive more power."

Laura Stratford, in her book *Satan's Underground,* also tells of her own childhood of sexual abuse and pornographic exploitation. As she grew up, the perversion took on a satanic focus, she says. Now a Christian, she tells of seeing torture, rape, all sorts of perversion and even human sacrifice. She talks of infants obtained specifically for ritual murder in honor of Satan.

HER TALE WOULD BE TOO HORRIBLE to believe were it not backed up by so many others.

In the southeastern U.S., as I write this, a 20ish Christian woman and ex-cultist is recovering from a nervous breakdown after years of not telling a dark secret that has haunted her for so long. She tells of — *during a year when she was a teenage runaway* — joining a cult, being made pregnant, being forced to carry the child, then being required to give it up for ritual use. She never saw the baby again.

In the March 1989 issue of *Moody Monthly* magazine, the story of 42-year-old Samantha Hoyer is so nightmarish that I won't repeat all of it here. As an infant, Sam and a twin sister were handed over to a satanic cult by her mother, a prostitute. The two lived in rural New Hampshire with 200 other children who were regular victims of midnight rituals centered around unspeakable abuse that included physical mutilation, sexual perversion and ceremonial murder.

For example, at age five, Sam had been sexually violated too many times to remember — frequently with strange objects. Then, one night, she and all the other children were forced to stand mute as one of the children was murdered.

It had happened before. But this time is was her twin sister — ritually sacrificed as the adults praised Satan. Little Sam was forced to join in the dance around the screaming, pleading victim — little Sam's constant companion and truest friend since the day they both were born.

"They put her on this little altar and they chopped her head off," Samantha recounted to the Christian magazine, her voice dropping into a childlike monotone. "I tried to put her head back, but it didn't match ..."

But she had witnessed the large cult's adults commit ceremonial slaughter before. And she would again.

AT AGE NINE, SAM AND A NUMBER of other children were chosen to be "tested" by the cult's adults to determine which of them might be trained up as the cult's future high priest and priestess.

Each young candidate for the priesthood was strapped to a cross. It was set aflame. All but two died as the dancing, circling cult members chanted — "delivering" the young souls to Satan's vengeance.

"[The flames] usually hit their hair first," remembered Sam, again slipping into an emotionless monotone as she told her story. The only surviving candidates were Sam and a little boy named Jeremy. The fires set to their crosses smoldered and died out — despite repeated attempts to rekindle the flames. As the ceremony erupted into a wild orgy, the two were released and hailed as the chosen ones.

What followed were eight more years of constant sexual abuse and horror that I wil not detail here. *A graphic example:* cannibalism became popular among the adults. As punishment, the children were starved for days, then given prepared flesh of a slain friend. The adults taught the kids that they gained the powers of anyone the group devoured.

At age 13, the sexually abused Sam finally was old enough to conceive and give birth. But she watched, powerless, as her newborn — delivered in the midst of a dark ceremony — was killed because the high priestess wanted it to be a boy.

Today Sam is a Christian — but is under psychiatric care. The horror of her childhood cannot be blotted out. *Please include her in your prayers.* She is the frequent target of terror tactics from members of the cult — who have vowed that she will denounce Jesus and return to them.

Such horrible tales!

Why do I drag you through such evil? On a much-publicized Geraldo Rivera TV special several women broke down as they told similar stories. One described giving up a little boy and a little girl for ritual murder. She was forced to plunge the knife into at least one other infant in a bloody sacrifice — and was warned that she could never tell about her dead little ones, since she, too, was guilty of murder.

Is all this this too terrible to be true? No. The stories are too similar. Sure, some may turn out to be hoaxes. But the testimony is growing in its sheer volume.

Jacquie Balodis, a former satanist in Garden Grove, California, tells of watching her two children sacrificed to Satan.

SEAN SELLERS, NOW ON DEATH ROW in the Oklahoma State Penitentiary, tells of murdering his parents as a sacrifice to Satan. Now a Christian, he recalls getting involved in the fantasy game *Dungeons and Dragons* at age 13, then at age 15 making friends with a witch — whom he believed could take him farther into the dark side than the game could.

She made him strip naked, lie on the floor and chant incantations — which the young teen found very exciting. Suddenly, he remembers, he realized he was surrounded by mighty forces of power and evil. He was thrilled, he recalls.

What followed were years of seeking more and more evil power from his dark master, Satan. Blasphemy and sacrilege were common, he says. Then, his group decided to get extra power by breaking each of the Ten Commandments one by one.

When it came time to kill someone, they picked their victim carefully — someone that society would not miss. They found a friendless, all-night convenience grocery clerk. They made friends with him and gained his trust. Then one night, they shot him to death with a pistol.

SEAN TELLS OF THE EXCITEMENT OF THE KILL. "We were dedicated to serving Satan — as dedicated as anybody could be to serving God. I was like an animal — cold — no mercy, no remourse. On the way home, we all laughed about it. We giggled about what we were getting into. It was *exciting*. We laughed that the stupid guy had trusted us. And that we had blown him to hell.

"I felt really cocky about killing that guy —   I had done it finally and had gotten away with it."

Then, one night, he added his own parents to the list. He went to them in their bedroom, placed a gun against their heads and sent them to meet their Maker. He trembles as he tells the story.

He awaits execution in Oklahoma's electric chair for their deaths. He doesn't claim that Satan made him do it. He chose to murder the people who gave him life. *They had to be sacrificed for his dark master*.

POLICE OFFICIALS WORLDWIDE are taking the growing problem of satanist crimes very seriously. "Satanism is a problem, it is growing and it will continue to be a problem," says Sgt. Jon Hinchliff, head of a special investigative division of the Minneapolis Police Department.

Larry Dunn, a sheriff's deputy in Washington state, says he has talked to more than 170 survivors of satanic cults, all of whom report seeing human sacrifices.

"If you send an undercover officer in," says Lt. Larry Jones of the Boise (Idaho) Police Department, "before he gets through the first recruiting party, he has to have sex with some 14-year-old girl or boy or smoke dope. I don't think I'd send someone in; you're just going to lose him."

History confirms the reality of such horror:

IN THE 1400s JOHN V, DUKE OF BRITTANY, got repeated complaints that the Baron of Retz was murdering children. Investigating, the Duke discovered the Baron and friends openly collected children to sacrifice in the Black Mass. In a black-draped chapel, black candles adorned a black-shrouded altar. On the altar lay a nude woman, a cross between her breasts and a chalice between her thighs. With a host stolen from a church, a defrocked priest said a blasphemous version of the Mass. The high point of the ceremony was the sacrifice of a child.

The sacrifice was believed to release tremendous psychic power. The Baron was executed after evidence was collected that he and his associates had murdered more than 100 children.

IN THE SEVENTEENTH CENTURY a French girl named Françoise Montespan paid a Parisian fortune-teller to arrange for a Black Mass. The objective: for Françoise to become the king's mistress. It worked. Louis XIV ditched a younger and — it is said — lovelier mistress for Madame de Montespan.

Then a new lovely caught Louis' eye. Another Black Mass was offered up to the evil powers. Once more Françoise held the king in her occult clutches. But Louis had a far-roving eye, and his interest in other ladies of Paris sent Françoise back to the fortune-teller again and again.

But parents of missing children — sacrificed to keep Françoise in the king's arms — prompted police to launch an investigation. Citizens rioted when the allegations were announced. Although she was never tried, Françoise was exiled by Louis to a convent for life. The fortune-teller and her associates were prosecuted. Before they were put to death, they confessed they had slaughtered 1,500 children.

SO DON'T THINK ALL THOSE WITCHES brought to trial in the Middle Ages were innocent, sweet old ladies victimized by religious nuts. Some of them may have been innocent, but there is increasing evidence that witchcraft itself is and always has been a horrible mixture of paganism, blasphemy, and murder.

You say that's all ancient history?

Witchcraft-related murder is commonplace today in rural Africa, according to author and former witchdoctor Credo Mutwa. Great power is believed to be held by medicines called *muti*. *Muti* requires human flesh, usually vital organs removed while the victim is still alive. South African police tell of a boy studying to become a witchdoctor, herding cattle with an eleven-year-old friend. Suddenly, he turned and cut her throat. He told officials he needed the liver of a friend so he could learn how to make *muti*.

In the Police Museum in the city of Pretoria, South Africa, various displays document recent cases of ritual murder and human sacrifice. One photo shows a three-year-old child, naked and spread-eagled, a large incision ripped in his stomach where his inner organs were removed.

DESPITE SUCH HORROR, today there are probably more people practicing witchcraft than ever before in history. Some may try it for a lark, but witchcraft is no joke today. It's dangerous and deadly.

In recent years a group of American teen-agers was found nailing hamsters to a cross and two New York boys beat a baby to death and tied it to a cross. A California school teacher was murdered and her heart and lungs used in a sacrifice to the devil, and a New Jersey boy was thrown into a pond as part of satanic ritual. In Florida, police reported that the battered, mutilated body of 17-year-old Mike Cochran was found outside of Daytona Beach, "the victim of devil worshippers, killed in a frenzied sacrificial ritual," according to an *Associated Press* news story.

In a highly publicized case in April, 1989, members of a Matamoros, Mexico, cult were arrested in the ritual murders of 12 people, including U.S. college student Mark Kilroy, whom they kidnapped during Spring Break from a bar. Victims' brains were put into a mixture of blood, herbs, rooster feet, goat heads and turtles. "We killed them for protection," said Elio Hernandez Rivera, 22, at a news conference called by police. He said cult members removed victims' vertebrae to use in necklaces.

"Very clearly, they believed the human sacrifices put a magical shield around them protected them from evil or harm, even up to bullets," said Texas Attorney General Jim Mattox.

IN DENVER, SATANISM IS very, very prevalent" among local teens, according to Jim McCarthy, director of the Bethesda PsychHealth center in the Colorado capital.

Officials of the Human Society nationwide have expressed concern over what one official called "the new fad of kids torturing animals as they play at this satanist stuff." In Orlando, Florida, a spokesman on the April 9, 1989, local TV evening news asked the public to report any incidents of animals being ritually abused — since the situation was "of growing concern to those of us who love animals."

ANTON SZANDOR LAVEY FOUNDED and heads what he calls the Church of Satan. At his church services vile practicies occur as the congregation hails the names of infernal deities.

LaVey has written *The Satanic Bible,* published by Avon Books in 1969 and still a bestseller.

It contains such choice words of wisdom as these:
• He who turns the other cheek is a cowardly dog.
• Say unto thine heart, "I am mine own redeemer."
• Blessed are the iron-handed, for the unfit shall flee before them
• Cursed are the poor in spirit, for they shall be spat upon.
• Satan represents all the so-called sins, as they all lead to physical, mental, or emotional gratification.

In his *Satanic Bible* LaVey glorifies Satan and ridicules Jesus and the Lord God. He extols the seven deadly sins and says it's only natural to indulge in lust, pride, greed, etc.

He takes everything in the Bible and reverses it with hellish logic. He tells you among other things how to sell your soul, how to choose a human sacrifice, how to pray to the devil, how to perform magic, and how to conjure lust and destruction of your enemies.

LaVey says it's stupid to go halfway into witchcraft. He's all for having all witches admit they're into evil and leave it at that. And while Satan worship isn't necessarily traditional witchcraft, I notice that most witches seem on pretty familiar terms with Satan.

SATAN'S GOSPEL DENIES THE REALITY OF GOD, of a Savior, of heaven — and even sneers at the idea that the devil and hell are real. It destroys true freedom and individualism and brotherhood and peace and love. It promises many of these things but provides only caricatures of them. Above all, it has no hope.

When the artist Michelangelo painted The Last Judgment, he pictured one man who is just beginning to realize he is in hell. His chin is sunk into his hand. His eyes are staring in the awful realization that he is lost forever. He knows now that there is no more hope for him anywhere, ever.

That is an accurate picture of the person who turns from the glorious Gospel of Christ to the garbled gospel of Satan.

For we have hope. *They do not!*

And they know it.

But here is a prediction:

In the next years, watch as satanists attempt to gain legal status and popular acceptance in the entertainment media — just as they have done so masterfully with our teens' heavy-metal rock music.

The legal battle has already been won quietly and without fanfare in the United States military where the Church of Satan is offially recognized as a "minority religion."

As I write this, the nation's prisons are under increasing legal assault, too, as satanists attempt to "protect the civil rights" of devil-worshiping inmates and bring in satanic chaplains and allow satanists to have the same access to prisoners as do Christian groups.

WHY HAVEN'T YOU HEARD ABOUT THIS? Because if it were accompanied by publicity, the good people of the United States would rise up in anger. So, it is happening quietly — and effectively. Already satanists are seeking official status as chaplains and counselors at hospitals and drug treatment facilities — particularly for adolescents.

I know of a hospital in Colorado where the infiltration has been even more subtle. A nurse in charge of one floor is a satanist. Although no devil worship occurs, Christians visiting her floor have come away shaken. Their spirits discerned something dark and terrible occurring — particularly around Halloween when the floor is elaborately decorated in an occult theme … which is strange since the other holidays do not merit such attention on that floor.

What can we do? Pray? *Of course*. But ask the Lord to empower you, to send you and to show you what must be done.

Be vigilant, my friends! Are the followers of Lucifer filling a void where you refuse to serve? Are you helping out in the community? In prison ministry? In state reform schools for youths? In the hospitals? In drug treatment programs?

Why not? We Christians have the only real answers for inmates, the sick and the addicted!

So, why are we abandoning the victims to Lucifer?

17

THE EVIL SEDUCTION

One of the first times

I went fishing was in a little stream near my father's house with two of my older brothers. Soon after we got there, I remember, I was slowly pulling in my line when I felt a big tug.

"Hey!" I shouted to my brother Gene. "I've got a big one!"

"You'd better wait and see what you've got," said Gene. He realized before I did what had happened.

My fishing line had caught on a tangle of someone else's lost line at the bottom of the stream. Just when I thought that was it, I discovered that the tangle of fishing line was caught on an old shoe, and the shoe was tied somehow to the inner tube from a tire! When the whole mess, dripping with mud, came out of the water, my two brothers laughed so hard they rolled on the ground.

I think of that now. Witchcraft is heavily involved with astrology and evil spirits.

Spiritualism leads on to the sort of demonic possession that my mother experienced throughout my childhood.

But the evil seduction has many forms in modern society.

ON THE TV IN MY HOTEL ROOM, a prominent book and magazine publishing company offers an exciting new book series Once every 6 weeks, you'll receive *in the comfort of your home* a new, exciting volume exploring the unknown worlds of the occult!

Do you see the danger of helping curious people begin to dabble in the dark arts? But it's everywhere we look!

Satanic bibles are available in your favorite shopping mall book shops. Books on tarot cards are in the public library. Dungeons and Dragons games can be bought by any eight-year-old in the toy stores.

In the supermarket, scandal-mongering tabloid newspapers are full of exciting "news" about the occult. Recently I was shown four trashy rags filled with such headlines as:

• *Star Talk from Beyond the Grave: Dead Celebrities Answer Readers' Letters Through Psychic Channelers*

• *Victim of satanic pregnancy ritual: Girl Has Baby With 2-ft Tail and Horns*

• *HEAVENLY MARRIAGE: Natalie Wood Is Wed to Elvis In World Beyond the Grave*

• *44 Women Sorcerers Have Power To Control The World*

• *Amazing Couple Can Look Into Heaven: Psychic Husband and Wife See Souls Returning to Their New Lives*

Everywhere, faith in this kind of stuff is becoming increasingly open. On U.S. Army bases, admitted satanists are in command of troops — for, as I mentioned before, satanism is a recognized "minority" religion in America's armed forces!

Why is there such interest in Satan's false hope?

After all, the fruit of his evil is always disappointing ... flawed ... twisted ... and brings with it horrible curses.

GOD WARNS THAT IF A PROPHET FORETELLS something and it doesn't happen, the prophet is not from God (Deuteronomy 18:21, 22). So, how can you detect a demonic prophet?

There are a number of ways.

Basically, anybody who sets themselves up as fortunetellers is denounced in a number of passages in the Bible. We are absolutely barred from having anything to do with anybody practicing magic, sorcery, witchcraft or fortune-telling.

But if such strong prohibitions from Almighty God are not good enough for you, notice the flawed, incomplete nature of the demonic supernatural. Look at the *National Enquirer* supermarket tabloid newspaper's 37 predictions for 1988. At the beginning of the year, they were very exciting. But how many came true? *One.* Thirty six were not even close. For example,

• The *Enquirer's* panel of 10 psychics said actor Clint Eastwood would seek the 1988 nomination to become the U.S. President.

• The psychics also said a presidential candidate would drop out of the race when it was revealed he was a transvestite (a man who likes disguising himself as a female).

• And they said Queen Elizabeth II of Great Britain would abdicate to become a housewife.

What prediction did the panel of psychics get *right?* That TV journalist Geraldo Rivera would be attacked on camera during one of his shows. *That one actually came true.* During a brawl between two angry groups of guests, one threw a chair at him, breaking his nose.

Keep reading Deuteronomy and you'll see that the 36 misses would have gotten the *Enquirer's* psychics stoned behind the city gates as false prophets!

Yet, modern man is fascinated by the glittering lies!

IN A HOTEL LOBBY IN MIAMI, I heard someone talking very enthusiastically behind a potted palm tree. When I walked around behind it, I saw an easel with a sign:

MADAME CONTESSA
Palmistry, Personal Counseling
Appointments Must Be Made In Advance

Near the sign a middle-aged woman with a dark turban on her head was holding the hand of a girl who looked about 20. "This summer," I heard her saying, "you will meet a man who will offer you unusual opportunities. He will become one of the most important men in your life. At first you may think this is just another date, but you will be mistaken."

"Now I see a crisis coming within the next two years. You will have to decide ..."

The occult seduces with the pleasing, pleasant and joyful. Then, gradually, insidiously it gets you in its grip. You may seek blessing, but you reap death and darkness.

Some are hooked by tarot cards. For some people Satan uses the *ouija* board. Drugs bring others in. A girl interviewed at a drug-abuse center in California said, "Before I came to the center I wasn't involved in witchcraft. But my friends were getting so heavily into getting high that when drugs didn't satisfy them, that's when they got into witchcraft."

In Denver, health specialist Jim McCarthy said the two groups at highest risk for joining satanist groups are children in institutions and teens with low self-esteem. They often get hooked through heavy-metal music and role-playing games such as *Dungeons and Dragons,* he said. He added that when drugs and role-playing games merge, the youth is in serious trouble. In one Denver-area case, two boys died because they thought they wouldn't be hurt if they were shot. Another boy jumped in front of a semi-trailer, believing the truck would pass right through him.

A college student in Indiana said: "Demon possession starts in lots of ways. I think it often begins with drugs or non-Christian meditation because when you're playing with your mind, it's very easy for the demons to get in."

A RECENT ISSUE OF A MAGAZINE for young people featured a long story about a boy who invoked Satan and found himself unable to keep from committing a series of ritual murders.

In the same magazine was an article about non-Christian forms of meditation and mind-control. It repeated testimonials from high school and college students about how wonderful they felt and how their school work had improved since they began practicing meditation. Some of the students said they got such good feelings from it that they no longer used drugs.

After this enthusiastic sales pitch for mystical types of meditation, the magazine listed places where classes are held, and for those not near enough to attend the classes it gave an address from which lessons could be bought by mail.

THAT MAKES ME ANGRY. If the same magazine listed the addresses of churches where young people could hear the liberating Gospel of Christ and — *if that's what they're interested in* — learn all about Christian meditation, you can imagine how many protests there would be. But who raises a word of protest when the public is urged to try a new, dark religion?

Beware of anyone who wants to teach you how to "unlock the secrets of your mind." Bring up the subject of Jesus. Find out where the person attends church. Then, ask your pastor what he thinks of their philosophy — and what does he know about their church. *Beware!* So much meditation calls on you to empty your mind. *Why?*

What's wrong with a full mind?

Max Gunther, a Connecticut writer who has done quite a bit of research into the occult, once talked with a man named Al Manning about how to get acquainted with your familiar spirit. Manning recommended *emptying the mind* so the spirit can make itself known to the consciousness!

ONE OF THE MOST POPULAR TRAPS is astrology. There's hardly a newspaper today without a daily horoscope — frequently on the comics pages, where kids get hooked.

At one newstand where paperbacks were sold I counted 48 books and 17 magazines — each with a different title — on astrology. Now you can even buy forecasts that are supposed to be run up by computers. One of the first things many strangers ask when they meet is *"What's your birth sign?"*

I would be the last person to say there is no truth in astrology. There seems to be increasing evidence that the phases of the moon are connected somehow with such things as the level of crime and the birth rate, and if the moon can affect human beings, maybe the planets do. But every part of the occult world has a grain of truth mixed with a ton of falsehood and a hundred tons of demonic lies, designed to get you out of God's control and into Satan's.

So if you get interested in astrology, you may very well find enough truth in it to lead you ever deeper into its spell.

TODAY, A PANDORA'S BOX OF HORROR has been released upon the world. In American and Canadian shopping malls, bookstores are full of its sinister delights. In British newsstands and U.S. supermarkets, tabloid newspapers tout its power.

In front of TVs, our next generation stares, hypnotized as cute little Smurfs and superheroes utter the cleverest magical incantations.

In our high schools, teens wear black, heavy-metal rock t-shirts proclaiming Satan's power. In our factories, workers learn to apply the wonders of Zen to their productivity. In our churches, senior citizens are taught Hindu techniques of relaxation and visualization.

Consider these facts:

• 3.8 million responding occultists' names are on the computerized mailing list of Informat, a California-based direct marketing agency that sells their addresses to companies that send out junk mail on occult books, magazines, charms, voodoo pendants and so forth.

• A multi-million-dollar bestseller at B. Dalton, Bookseller and Waldenbooks and other shopping mall bookstores across the United States is *The Satanic Bible* by Anton LaVey, founder of San Francisco's Church of Satan.

- Recently, the American Astrological Association reported sales of personalized horoscopes to 339,660 individuals willing to pay up to $9.95 for their very own daily advice.

It's here.

It's thriving.

And it's demonic.

In the streets

of San Francisco and Los Angeles, witches march, demanding the right to practice their rites openly. In Louisiana graves are opened and bodies looted so demon worshipers can make necklaces of human finger bones. In Iowa and Ohio, cattle are mutilated — ears and tails removed, blood drained for use in satanic ceremonies. In New York tombstones are broken. In Indiana churches are desecrated with spray-painted demonic symbols.

In big cities, those who attempt to help runaway children say that now the kids are not only preyed upon by drug dealers and homosexual molesters, but by a growing number of Lucifer worshipers who see the youngsters as a good source of human bodies for sexual and sacrificial rites. These sorts of kids vanish all the time, anyway, so a few more suddenly missing off the streets aren't going to be reported.

Canadian Mounted Police Constable James Brown reported evidence linking satanism to unsolved disappearances of several Alberta, Canada, children. He went on to declare "children have a strong significance in satanic rituals and there are suggestions they may be used in sacrifices."

AND ALTHOUGH WE IN THE CHRISTIAN, western part of the world have been protected for years from the hideousness of true paganism, it is still strong — *and as demonic as ever!*

Throughout India and Tibet, the devout pray to various devil images, many of which represent real demon spirits that take a horrible, active part in local events.

In Africa and undeveloped parts of Asia and South America, witches and sorcerers are incredibly common — and are not merely something on America's Saturday morning children's TV.

In Central America's largest republic — Guatemala — Indian witch doctors are preaching prophecies that the native population would be in servitude to the whites for only 500 years — then the mystic god-kings of the Mayan and Aztec empires will rise again! Well, Columbus came in 1492. The 500th anniversary of the age of the conquistadors coincides with the turn of the century — the year 2000!

All across the Islamic world, millions upon millions from Indonesia to Morocco bow down repeatedly each day to their false, demonic god who promises them instant immortality in heaven *if they die murdering a Christian or Jew!* If you observe much of modern-day Islam, you may come to the conclusion that their god, Allah, may be the Prince of Persia as described in detail in the 11th chapter of Daniel. How can anybody think so?

Look at the havoc that this small region of the world wreaks on international politics! Repeatedly the tiny country of Iran (modern-day Persia) has brought America to its knees — ending Jimmy Carter's presidency, murdering hundreds of U.S. civilians and soldiers in terrorist bombings and sneak attacks.

Although communism is a terrible, godless horror in many parts of the world, I believe Islam will spread far worse problems. For years, communism and Islamic terrorism have worked together against Christianity and the state of Israel.

But I suspect the communists are being manipulated — *used* — as part of a larger scheme that will not fulfill their plans for world domination at all. The Moslem population in the large Asian portions of the Soviet Union continues to outnumber the Christian and atheist European Soviets. We may see more dramatic changes in Russia and an entirely unexpected reason for the Soviets to become the Magog of Revelation!

HOW DO WE FIGHT BACK? Just as we have for 2,000 years! With the truth of our salvation! With the wonderful message of Jesus' love! With John 3:16! Evangelism! Once, Europe was completely pagan. Then, Christianity grew ... and today has waned. Well, it can be nurtured again!

Once Russia was a mighty Christian nation.

Well, it can be again. *And so can America.*

So, don't listen when friends want to tell about their astrologer or fortune-teller or palm-reader who each week foretells such exciting things that *usually* come to pass. Shun such talk! Witness Jesus Christ to your friend. If they won't give up their evil conversation be blunt: *further witchcraft talk will end your friendship!*

Why? John 16:13 tells us plainly: "He will guide you into all truth ... and he will show you things to come. " That means only God is permitted to let any human being peek ahead into the future.

He has allowed only a few prophets and other men of God this rare privilege. If we get tired of waiting for God to show us the future and decide to seek such secrets from the forces of evil, we get ourselves into big trouble. That is, if we don't care to follow God's way, there is only one alternative: Satan's.

There's nothing in between God and Lucifer. There is no such thing as a "white witch" — despite what you may hear from the false prophets of TV talk shows. "Good witches" really hate Christ. They are jealous of the great power of His holy Name. They know that they wield only deception and darkness from Satan. And in the final battle, they know, they are doomed to complete defeat.

BUT WHAT ABOUT WELL-MEANING RELATIVES who buy your kids fun games such as *ouija* boards, tarot cards or the fantasy role-playing games where your children pretend to have evil powers — just for "fun?" Burn those games. Forbid your children to play them at friends' houses.

Go through your children's music albums. So much of heavy metal rock is filled with adoration of Satan. In Sackville, Nova Scotia, Canada, 16 year old Derek Shaw called his girlfriend and told how after months of listening to satanic music, Lucifer had just appeared to him in a blue light and demanded his soul. He hung up, went to his parents' bedroom, took down his father's rifle, put the barrel in his mouth and killed himself.

In Jefferson Township, New Jersey, 14-year-old Thomas Sullivan Jr., after weeks of studying the occult and listening to heavy metal rock, according to the *Chicago Tribune,* murdered his mother with a three-inch knife, hideously defacing her body before slitting his own throat ear-to-ear and drowning in his own blood.

Secular psychiatrist, Dr. Khalil Ahmad, director of adolescent services at Dartmouth, notes the relationship of many youthful disturbances to the demon-glorifying lyrics filling their minds: "Teenagers are looking for excitement," he said. "The weak-willed, often the losers, are attracted to satanism. It gives them a false impression of power."

WHAT ABOUT NATIVE RELIGIONS of the American west, the Australian aborigine or New Zealand's Maoris? Each is just as evil and demonic as any other pagan cult that repudiates Jesus Christ. Don't be lulled into thinking there's cultural richness in drinking native herbs or having visions in a sweat lodge.

The same goes for seemingly mind-broadening experiences as a "free Hindi meal" put on by Hare Khrishna cultists visiting university campuses. *Beware!* At most of these, an opportunity comes for you to politely bow down to the blue-skinned demon god-boy Khrishna.

Don't go!

We Christians stick out like a sore thumb in such places anyway! The joy of Jesus radiates from us and blinds the evil demon followers — infuriating them, torturing them. They know that the power we have within us and all around us is *so much more mighty* than any deceptive tool of hate that they can wield!

I remember vividly the hatred I felt for David Wilkerson. The demonic forces in my life cried out their anger against his supernatural anointing from God's Holy Spirit.

A Christian's very presence makes many occultists furious — envious in a horrible, deadly way! *Vengeful!* By going, you set yourself up as a target — either for violence or intense recruitment.

So, do we hide in terror of some naughty demon-worshipper who might hurt us? *No!* Praise God that David Wilkerson did not!

WE ARE SUPPOSED TO BE SPIRITUAL WARRIORS, clothed in righteous armor, excited about going into battle! Don't fool around with magic, astrology, reincarnation, gu-rus, spiritualism, inner visions, mystic auras, astral travel, *ouija* , witchcraft, or anything of the kind. All of it is from below, not from above — from the devil, not from God.

Ban it from your home.

Rid your personal library of books about witches and sorcery and magical spells.

Turn off the TV.

And prepare yourself for battle!

As the twentieth century hurtles toward its end, I believe we are going to see stranger and stranger things. In 2 Thessalonians there is a remarkable passage about the return of Christ:

"*...that day shall not come, except there come a falling away first, and that man of sin be revealed, the son of perdition; Who opposeth and exalteth himself above all that is called God, or that is worshiped; so that he as God sitteth in the temple of God, shewing himself that he is God*" (2 Thessalonians 2:3, 4).

Paul is saying that Christ will not come again until there is first a falling away. "Falling away" may mean either a falling away from the Christian faith or a great final rebellion — or both. Who is the man of sin who will be revealed before Christ returns? Notice that he is called "the son of perdition" and will proclaim that he is God and will oppose God and exalt himself above Him.

THERE ARE MANY DIFFERENT INTERPRETATIONS of Bible passages such as these and I don't want to get into a discussion of them. What impresses me is how this fits in with what we are already seeing happening. Rebellion and unbelief are everywhere. It is fashionable and hip to oppose God and everything related to God. And already Satan himself is worshipped in place of God in so-called churches of Satan, while the devil and his angels are invoked in witchcraft covens all around the world.

Paul goes on: *"For the mystery of iniquity doth already work: only he who now letteth will let, until he be taken out of the way. And then shall that Wicked be revealed, whom the Lord shall consume with the spirit of his mouth, and shall destroy with the brightness of his coming: Even him, whose coming is after the working of Satan with all power and signs and lying wonders, And with all deceivableness of unrighteousness in them that perish; because they received not the love of the truth, that they might be saved"* (verses 7-10).

I like the way the Living Bible translates that:

As for the work this man of rebellion and hell will do when he comes, it is already going on, but he himself will not come until the one who is holding him back steps out of the way. Then this wicked one will appear, whom the Lord Jesus will burn up with the breath of his mouth and destroy by his presence when he returns. This man of sin will come as Satan's tool, full of satanic power, and will trick everyone with strange demonstrations, and will do great miracles. He will completely fool those who are on their way to hell because they have said "no" to the Truth; they have refused to believe it and love it, and let it save them.

The wicked one who is coming will carry on a work that had already begun in the time of the New Testament. But through the ages God has been holding Satan back. At the end of this age, He will step out of the way and for a few years a man full of sin, a tool of Satan with satanic power, will fool everyone who does not really believe and love God's saving truth.

Such people will believe lies and strong delusions.

SUCH AS THE OCCULT. What else is filled with deception, delusions, and demonstrations of seemingly miraculous power? As this age rolls on, I believe such demonstrations will become more and more convincing to everyone except those who are close to Jesus.

I predict that in a short time another new religion will sweep across much of the world. Maybe it will be a mixture of witchcraft, spiritualism, and some Eastern religion. It wouldn't surprise me if it had elements of Christianity in it. That way it would fool a lot of half-committed Christians. What shape it will take exactly I don't know, but I feel sure that the time is ripe for some new delusion.

The only ones who will be completely safe in the times ahead of us are the Christians who love Jesus and live 100 percent for Him.

All others will become easy prey for that old serpent who has been a liar and murderer *from the beginning of time!*

18

HOW DO WE ATTACK SATAN?

Evangelism!

These cultists are trying to win the world! Well, folks, Jesus was quite clear in His orders to us, too. Winning the world is *OUR* job. So, instead of letting the forces of evil recruit your friends, hit your buddies first!

You *would* like to spend eternity with your friends, wouldn't you? Won't it be *great* to run into an old friend when you get to heaven and have to be *humble* as he announces to everybody that *you're* the reason he gave his heart to Jesus? Or are you running the risk on Judgment Day of friends turning to you in horror — *as they are condemned to eternal damnation* — and demanding to know why you never said anything?

MAYBE YOU'RE BOLD ENOUGH to take your attack to the very gates of hell — and want to do some heart-to-heart witnessing to known cultists.

It works! In another chapter, I will tell the story of Annie and a Satan-worshiper named Miguel. If she hadn't shared her beliefs with Miguel, he might never have heard the truth. Go get the help of some *solid* Christians and go to work on the deluded devil-followers! *How?*

Just like when I was a street fighter! I didn't ever pick a fight with 20 armed guys from an enemy gang! *No!* I picked my opponents wisely.

And I *outnumbered* them whenever possible.

I liked winning. So should you.

There's nothing wrong with five good Christian believers lying in ambush for someone caught in the lies of Hare Khrishna. But remember that we have to do everything in *love!* You can't force anybody to accept Jesus as their personal Savior. Remember, your goal is not to win a debate.

You want to win their heart. *You want them to become your brother.*

HERE'S HOW BILLY GRAHAM handled a series of attacks by avowed satanists determined to disrupt his crusades. He tells about it in his book *Approaching Hoofbeats: The Four Horsemen of the Apocalypse:*

"Three hundred Satan worshipers approached our crusade in Chicago with the specific intent of taking over the platform and stopping the crusade service, which was in progress. They announced their plan in advance, but I didn't dream they would actually try to storm the platform.

"We had just sung the second hymn of the evening. George Beverly Shea had sung a gospel song and Cliff Barrows was about to lead a massed choir in a great anthem of praise. At that moment, a policeman rushed to the stage and whispered something in the ear of the mayor of Chicago, who was present that night to welcome us.

"At the same moment, the Satan worshipers forced their way past the ushers at the rear of that spacious auditorium and were proceeding down the back aisles toward the platform. There were more than 30,000 young people in that Youth Night service. Only those seated near the back saw the Satan worshipers enter. The mayor of Chicago turned to me and said, 'Dr. Graham, we'll let the police handle these intruders.'

"WE NEVER CALL IN THE POLICE for crusade duty if we can help it. 'Let me try another way, Mr. Mayor,' I suggested. I interrupted the choir's song and addressed the 30,000 young people in McCormick Place. 'There are about 300 Satan worshipers entering the auditorium. They say they are going to take over the platform. You can hear them coming now.'

"The crowd could hear the rising chant of the Satan worshipers. Everyone turned to see them moving with determination down the aisles, past the ushers who were working to restrain them. They were causing a considerable disturbance by then. I continued addressing the crowd. 'I'm going to ask you Christian young people to surround these Satan worshipers,' I exhorted. 'Love them. Pray for them. Sing to them. And gradually ease them back toward the entrances through which they have come."

"I WILL NEVER FORGET THAT MOMENT! Hundreds of young Christians stood to their feet and did exactly as I had asked. Some grabbed

hands and began to sing. Others put their arms around the Satan worshipers and began to pray for them. Others calmly shared their faith with them. Everyone else in McCormick Place sat praying as God's Spirit moved through His people to confound the work of Satan in our midst. I stood watching in silence. I waited and prayed until peace was restored and the service could resume.

"It happened again in Oakland, California, in the football stadium. Hundreds of Satan worshipers again invaded the meeting to distract and disturb thousands who had come to hear of Christ and His plan of salvation. We did the same thing we had done in Chicago. Again, hundreds of Christians stood and gently led the worshipers of Satan from the stadium.

"I asked the young people to surround them and love them. They did! Later that week, I received a letter from one of the leaders of the satanist group thanking me for what I had done. He wrote, 'I think you saved our lives.' The power of those Christian young people came not in the impact of evil and violent force, but in their quiet, loving prayerful resolution."

PLOT YOUR STRATEGIES WELL. Then attack in love, armed with truth! Plant a seed. You may not be there to harvest it, but somebody has to tell that Moonie kid or the Jehovah's Witness lady or the door-to-door Mormon missionaries the truth about a mighty God who sent His son to save us from all the lies they believe in.

Yes, we are permitted to fight back!

What a joy when a group of strong, committed Christian kids goes to a rock concert to pass out tracts and witness! I've seen this and it's almost funny: the good Christian kids look like aliens amid the swirl of evil! The music is so awful and degrading that they usually retreat outside.

That's OK since it's much more effective for them to wait outside anyway, where the empty, hurting concert-goers leaving the orgy of evil will see a ray of hope — a bright-and-shining promise — thrusting a tract at them, grinning and assuring them that Jesus loves them.

I ENCOURAGE YOU TO GO WITNESSING at a rock concert. Be sure to go in strength — in numbers. You're a spiritual street fighter!

Go with experienced, effective street-witnesses and you'll be astonished at how many kids and adults will come to know the Lord right there on the sidewalk! Sure, you may be ridiculed by an occasional scoffer, but it's worth it! *That's what the Christian life is all about!*

What we believe becomes what we *are!* We can't hide it!

Does Philippians 4:8 — which orders us to keep our minds on good, lovely and pure things — mean we are just supposed to think about pretty flowers and beautiful sunsets? *Should we ignore evil?* Well, keep reading your Bible with me:

THE APOSTLE PAUL WAS INSPIRED BY GOD to put down this mighty warning in II Thessalonians 2:3-15:

"...First, there will be a time of great rebellion against God, then the man of rebellion will come — the son of hell. He will defy every god there is, and tear down every other object of adoration and worship. He will go in and sit as God in the temple of God, claiming that he himself is God. Don't you remember that I told you this when I was with you? And you know what is keeping him from being here already, for he can come only when his time is ready.

"As for the work this man of rebellion and hell will do when he comes, it is already going on, but he himself will not come until the one who is holding him back steps out of the way. Then this wicked one will appear, whom the Lord Jesus will burn up with the breath of his mouth and destroy by his presence when he returns. This man of sin will come as Satan's tool, full of satanic power, and will trick everyone with strange demonstrations, and will do great miracles. He will completely fool those who are on their way to hell because they have said 'no' to the Truth; they have refused to believe it and love it, and let it save them, so God will allow them to believe lies with all their hearts, and all of them will be justly judged for believing falsehood, refusing the Truth, and enjoying their sins..."

Yes, the Bible tells us that terrible things are coming.

So, are we to ignore that possibility? Are we to flit about like happy little Christian butterflies, singing Psalms and clouding up if someone says something mean to us? *No!* We're to be *warriors!*

WE'RE SUPPOSED TO FIGHT BACK! How? The answer is in Ephesians 6:10-12: *"...I want to remind you that your strength must come from the Lord's mighty power within you. Put on all of God's armor so that you will be able to stand safe against all strategies and tricks of Satan. For we are not fighting against people made of flesh and blood, but against persons without bodies — the evil rulers of the unseen world, those mighty satanic beings and great evil princes of darkness who rule this world; and against huge numbers of wicked spirits in the spirit world."*

And what is the armor that we must put on? I suspect you're already quoting the familiar checklist that follows in Ephesians 6:14-18:

"• You will need the strong belt of truth and

"• *The breastplate of God's approval.*

"• *Wear shoes that are able to speed you on as you preach the Good News of peace with God.*

"• *In every battle you will need faith as your shield to stop the fiery arrows aimed at you by Satan.*

"•*And you will need the helmet of salvation and*

"• *The sword of the Spirit — which is the Word of God.*

"• *Pray all the time. Ask God for anything in line with the Holy Spirit's wishes. Plead with him, reminding him of your needs, and keep praying earnestly for all Christians everywhere.*"

There are over 100 million followers of spiritism worldwide, reports Andreas Resch, director of the Institute for Para-Science in Austria.

As I travel across the world, I keep hearing terrible rumors of attempts by satanists to infiltrate church groups. I have good friends who tell how they have seen the evil effect of one well-placed satanist exercising dark power in such places as hospital wards and motion picture production companies. One story tells of a cult that has attempted to snatch Christian babies from church nurseries. In West Germany, the Bishops Conference of the United Protestant-Lutheran Church has issued sharp warnings against the occult.

God has given us clear guidelines, too:

"Don't be teamed with those who do not love the Lord, for what do the people of God have in common with the people of sin? How can light live with darkness? And what harmony can there be between Christ and the devil?" (II Cor. 6:14, 15).

It is here that we have to be so careful! The devil loves to twist this truth and cause such dissension between Christian brothers! Of course we cannot ignore this verse.

We must be on guard. The occult world is many-headed, and every head sprouts from a single source — Satan.

But we have the weapons to defeat him!

And he knows it.

Expect to win.

How? One way is by wooing back the deceived followers of the dark side. Every one of them is loved by God.

You could be responsible for their making it to heaven instead of being tortured in hell for eternity by their evil master.

How can you reach a satanist?

• **THROUGH THE POWER OF THE HOLY SPIRIT!** Pray! Seek the Lord's guidance before you charge into battle. Ask the Lord to show you who to talk to. Ask Him to miraculously give you the powerful words you'll need in spiritual hand-to-hand combat.

If Dave Wilkerson had battled me in his own power, using clever human wisdom, I would never have feared him. But, I was scared to death of him because I recognized the supernatural power that came from him — which I did not know was the might of the Holy Spirit. Instead, I was convinced that Dave was a powerful witch!

Remember, too, that hour upon hour in the loneliness of Satan's terrible spiritual counterassault against him, Dave diligently and faithfully sought the Lord's guidance.

His words "Nicky, Jesus loves you," were not powerful in themselves. But by the might of the Holy Spirit, they haunted me, almost driving me out of my mind. That message was exactly what I needed to hear. Dave could not have known it. But God's Holy Spirit did.

And you'll be given the right words in your time of battle — if you will ask the Lord to give them to you.

• **EMPHASIZE THE LOVE AND FORGIVENESS** of our mighty God, unless the Spirit directs you to the contrary. I can tell you that over and over I have seen love break through when condemnation won't.

So, don't hammer away on sin and damnation unless the Lord directs you specifically. Fire and brimstone messages worked for such great preachers as the colonial Puritan Jonathon Edwards or Billy Sunday. But it's not the message that works for me. Occultists often *know* they are condemned. Some take great pride in it — and will declare that they are destined to be powerful commanders of tens of thousands when they get to hell.

Others may even humbly agree with you that they are no good. *They think God hates them*. Most believe it's too late for them to turn back from their great evil.

But that's a *lie* that you can dispute in the power of the Lord's anointing if you will only seek His power. If Peter can boldly preach God's loving plan to the Sanhedrin, if Paul can look the Romans in the eye and tell them of Jesus' mercy, then you can, too, filled with God's Spirit.

If David Wilkerson had come in his own human power and preached damnation to me, I would have laughed in his face and possibly plunged a knife into his skinny ribs — right there in front of everybody!

I knew I was going to hell. I'd accepted it long ago. After all, I was the "Son of Satan" with the "Mark of the Beast" on my heart, in the words of my own mother. She was a respected *espiritista* who knew about such things, in my opinion.

• **DON'T PUSH SUBMISSION.** Cult members often have had their fill of that. Their leaders have shoved obedience down their throats. In fact, many cult members have lived under the total control of evil people who treated them like animals and subjected them to terrible degradations.

Some of these folks have been forced to kill their children in horrible ceremonies. Others have had to shout their approval as their little daughters were ritually raped or their wives sexually abused on the satanic altar. Their feelings of self-worth are lower than you can believe. You must show them the freedom that God gives us. Show how God wants us to have a free will and that He gives each one of us the ability to make our own decisions — particularly the decision to accept Jesus' love and salvation.

• **GO SLOWLY.** Don't be guilty of assembly-line religion. A friend of mine deeply involved in evil was approached by a Christian on a university campus. My friend sat and listened to the sales pitch, accepted the Lord, was given a handful of tracts, then was dumped as the Christian walked off in search of another prospect. My friend was so infuriated that he did not really become a faithful follower for several more years. And he still speaks of resentment of the egotistical "head-hunter" who was only interested in adding scalps to his belt, not souls for the Kingdom.

In school, teachers are sometimes pressured to let the curriculum dictate their teaching pace. If the teaching plan requires moving on to multiplication, even though the kids still don't grasp addition, too bad! The curriculum cannot be changed. As a result, kids are left behind in the dust. Don't be guilty of the same with a prospective Christian. Listen to their responses.

Just because you have a timetable for his salvation and Christian growth doesn't mean God does. Don't ram the Bible down your would-be convert's throat. Let him see the love of Jesus through your caring, non-judgmental attitude and example.

Listen. *Don't debate.* Love.

Constantly seek the Lord. As the battle progresses, you will need to hear from your Commander. Listen to Him. Don't let your successes on the battlefront go to your head, either.

He, alone, is God.

You are not.

• **EXPECT TO WIN GREAT VICTORIES.** It *will* happen. You are going to plant a lot of seeds. I have heard stories of cult members who encountered a loving Christian who turned their lives completely upside down. Although they might not have fallen to their knees in repentance right then and there, the witness of God's love echoed in their mind for weeks, months and even years. I know of one satanist abused in a horrible cult from her infancy who made friends with a Christian at age 10 and learned to call upon the name of Jesus for help.

Although she did not come to the Lord for another 25 years, she knew where to find rescue when she finally wanted it.

Yes, you are going to win.

And you are going to rescue a Charles Manson.

Or an Anton LaVey.

Or a Nicky Cruz.

19

WHAT IF YOU LEAD A WITCH TO JESUS?

What a joy

if will be when you are blessed into making sure that a witch will be in heaven! An *ex-witch* who loves Jesus, that is.

But what happens next when you lead a witch or a satanist or a Mormon or a Moonie to the Lord? What if you find yourself suddenly a brother with a defector from the dark side?

Be prepared for the ultimate test of your faith. Satan does not give up his own without a fight. So, dig in for a longterm commitment to this new Christian — who has put his or her faith in Jesus, but also in *you*. They're going to need your support.

They are going to need *you*. *Be there*.

SOME EX-CULTISTS WILL BE DELIVERED immediately from the evil tentacles of hell. My Mama was — and the Lord equipped her with a sound mind to battle the evil forces which came against her — as I will describe in a later chapter.

But some will take years before they recover fully. My Papa was so frightened of the evil powers ready to attack him and our family that even as a 70-year-old man, he did not believe he could survive the resulting assault if he declared his allegiance to Jesus Christ — a story I'll tell in a later chapter, too.

Don't be judgmental of the ones who are not healed immediately. Don't be disappointed if your convert's faith is not mighty and bold while he is still a newborn Christian.

Some miracles take time.

Some healings require patience.

Remember the story of the blind man of Bethsaida — told in Mark 8:22-26?

Jesus healed him of his blindness, but although the man suddenly could see, everything was apparently severely out of focus. So, Jesus laid hands on him a second time.

Only then was the man's sight perfect.

SOMETIMES GOD HAS A LESSON IN MIND for you and me, or whomever is put in a position to be His human instrument of healing and restoration. Remember the story of the demon-filled boy in Mark 9? The disciples failed in casting out the evil spirit.

When the boy was brought to the Lord, the child suddenly rolled in the dirt, foaming at the mouth.

Instead of moving quickly, Jesus quizzed the father about the affliction. When Jesus finally commanded the demon to leave, "… the demon screamed terribly and convulsed the boy again and left him;" says Mark 9:26. "and the boy lay there limp and motionless, to all appearance dead. A murmur ran through the crowd—'He is dead.'"

But Jesus took the boy by the hand and helped him to his feet. The boy was alive and restored to his right mind.

IMAGINE NOW, THE MIGHTY POWER OF JESUS — God with us, the Creator in the flesh, the only sinless man, our Messiah, conceived of the Holy Spirit, the Lamb of God sent to take away the sins of the world. If it took such effort on His part in these two healings, what will it require of us?

Indeed, when the disciples asked Him afterward why they had been unable to cast out the boy's demon, Jesus told them "This kind cannot be driven out by anything but prayer and fasting" (Mark 9:29.)

So, when you win Satan's vicious human followers to Jesus, be prepared to continue the battle. Take your petitions before Almighty God, seeking your convert's immediate healing, restoration and deliverance from the horrible evil that has hurt them so.

But don't be devastated if the Lord wants to teach you something — such as patience or compassion or the reality of laying down your life.

Sometimes a cultist is saved, but not completely restored to his or her right mind, or is not filled with immediate, mighty faith with which to battle Satan's counterattack.

What should you expect as you shepherd the defector?

1. YOUR CONVERT MAY BE SCARED TO DEATH of what's going to happen next. They may fear immense demonic forces that may be launched against them and their loved ones.

So be armed with scriptures about how the evil cannot touch us! Claim those scriptures just like Jesus did in the wilderness! Quote them at Satan, reminding him that *you know* that he cannot touch you or this new child of God.

Your ex-cultist may know that his former friends back in the coven or cult or satanic church may try to take vengeance against him. If you convert a believer from even such a non-violent cult as the Jehovah's Witnesses or the Mormons, expect the new Christian to be assaulted on every side by the members of his former congregation. Lovingly, then threateningly, they will try every persuasion possible to bring him back to their fellowship. If he does not return, he will be shunned — declared dead. His old friends will be barred from having anything to do with him. His wife and children may be forced to leave him. He may lose his job if he works for a member of his old cult.

If your convert was a member of a violent cult that practiced blood rituals and illegal acts — and if your defector has been a participant in or witness to murder, cannibalism, human sacrifice, sexual abuse of children — you may need to take measures to protect his life. He is a potential witness in court. His story told to the news media might open the public's eyes to the nightmarish threat in their community.

Thus, he is extremely dangerous to the leaders and members of his former cult — as well as to Satan, who the Bible tells us is proud and responds viciously to ridicule and humiliation. Satan wants to be respected and worshiped — not exposed as a murderer destroying little innocents and the souls of his most faithful followers.

Don't be surprised if you have to take measures to protect the physical safety of a former cultist. Death pacts may be sworn against them — to keep them from violating their vows of secrecy. Intimidation is common, scaring the defector into returning to the fold. You may need to help get your convert out of town. Or you may need the help of a large group of Christians to be with the escapee 24 hours a day.

2. YOU MAY NEED TO ENLIST OTHER CHRISTIANS as you work with a defector. Standing by your convert may be incredibly draining — spiritually, physically and emotionally.

At the first sign of such an ordeal ahead, don't try to be a Lone Ranger. If you need help, get it. As I mentioned earlier, when I was warlord of the Mau Maus, I never attacked a group of rival street fighters singlehandedly. I took 200 guys with me. I made sure we had ambushes, reinforcements, escape routes and secret weapons caches lined up.

Plot your battle plan the same way, remembering that we are not fighting against flesh and blood, but against evil spirit powers over which we are guaranteed victory. This is a battle. Use the tools the Lord gives you to win! Too much is at stake here.

I am ashamed to say that I hear stories of Christians who get involved with redeemed ex-cultists, but then back out of their commitment because of the patience, time and emotional investment required.

I have seen it over and over elsewhere, too. The patient doesn't get well immediately, so, the Christian throws up his hands, declares the victim doesn't have enough faith or is harboring secret sin. Then like a modern-day pharisee, the Christian struts away, his face filled with a disappointed, self-righteous scowl.

And a baby Christian is left crying in the jungle! **Alone!**
Undefended as Satan's jackals move in for the kill!

Even without their attack, a trusted Christian throwing in the towel can be devastating to the defector. Many followers of the dark arts have lived through years of betrayal and abandonment from the very members of their evil cult. Selfishness is a part of that way of life! It's vicious.

Furthermore, for years, they've been told that Christians are hypocrites and liars. So, now, *you* have shown them the truth of their loving Father. They have grabbed onto this last ray of hope.

They believe. Oh, how they believe!
And they may expect you to be perfect.

Yes, that's hard! But shown the hope of holiness, a convert may expect you to be the perfect Christian that he or she wants to become. The demand is too much on you, of course. You are human, too. But you must hang in there, seeking the Lord for the help you desperately need to lead this new believer to put his eyes on Jesus instead of you!

3. DON'T HURRY to turn your new friend into a Christian celebrity. The press may give him or her enormous publicity. All sorts of speaking engagements may come up. But what would have happened to you if you'd been declared an expert on Christianity two days after you were saved? Could you have defended yourself on *Donohue* or the *CBS Evening News?*

Worse than that, however, the new convert may handle himself or herself beautifully ... and seemingly mature overnight into a spiritual leader. Be careful! Skipping Christian babyhood is not healthy. We have to crawl before we can walk or run. Instant celebrity status can go to a new believer's head and destroy his or her witness.

Also, there is a Christian celebrity circuit out there that must be approached with caution. It's wonderful to have your testimony put into a book. It's exciting to be hurried onto all the Christian TV talk shows, then to be set up for nationwide appearances, complete with T-shirts bearing your face, a movie based on your life, and Christian groupies screaming your name and pleading for you to autograph their Bibles.

But how can a baby Christian survive all that? I can rattle off a list of young believers I've seen eaten alive by instant celebrity status. Rock singers. Movie stars. *Ex-Mau Maus.*

4. BE OPEN AND CARING TO YOUR CONVERT. Frankly, he may be a bit of a social misfit. Such folks are exactly the sort that cults target for recruitment — people with problems, few friends, poor social skills ... seeming rejects of society. Remember that Jesus took 12 misfits — a bunch of illiterate fishermen, tax collectors and miscellaneous unemployed country boys — and turned the world upside down.

Tradition has it that Mary Magdalene was a street prostitute before Jesus found her. She became a mighty witness — so bold that when all the men deserted and even Peter cursed aloud the very thought that he followed Jesus, she was right there at the foot of the cross, unafraid, ready to die with Him.

Your convert may have been through horrors you cannot begin to believe — such as ritual abuse since childhood. Be there for them. Be prepared to provide food, clothing and, particularly, a caring home. You may be in this for the long haul. You may have to help your defector establish a new life. But remember that Jesus didn't forgive Mary Magdalene, then tell her to hit the road and figure out her own problems.

But what if the satanist or young dabbler in the occult that you're trying to lead to Jesus ...is your own child?

And what if he or she isn't interested in Christ?

20

How can parents fight for their kids?

Recently a woman called me

from Oklahoma. "I'm Jean Hawthorn. I have three children, and I was so disturbed today when my daughter in junior high brought home that old book, *Rosemary's Baby*. Her English class is reading it for some reason. What can we parents do to protect our children from things like this?"

I don't remember all that I told Mrs. Hawthorn, but right here I want to say how important it is for parents to know what is happening today and to work to protect young people from one of Satan's worst mass onslaughts in centuries. Between drugs, pornography, and today's flood of occultism, our young people won't have a chance unless adults do all in their power to help them survive.

REFUSE TO HAVE CERTAIN THINGS IN YOUR HOME — items that I have already mentioned in this book: horoscopes, *Dungeons and Dragons,* books on the supernatural. Get rid of idols, too.

Idols? The pagan Canaanites of the Old Testament believed their evil images had enormous power. God considered them a vile abomination. The Israelites were supposed to burn them — and not even recover the melted gold or silver!

You may have idols in your home that you don't recognize. How about Mexican figurines? These cute curios may be copies of evil Aztec demon-gods to whom virgins were sacrificed! How about cute little, fat Buddha lamps. *Harmless?* No! Buddha is a *false* god. Millions of souls throughout Asia are headed straight to hell because they put their trust in his teachings instead of Jesus Christ.

EVANGELIST JAMES ROBISON once helped a prominent Texas millionaire destroy hundreds of thousands of dollars of ancient idols that the oilman had collected from throughout the world.

They discarded valuable gold, silver and ivory.

One of the set of idols, they learned, had been commissioned by a Chinese emperor who, after the sculptor finished the images, had the artist executed, so that the images would be one of a kind.

A good friend of mine — a Christian book publisher — had accumulated a number of statues of the Mayan, Aztec and Toltec god called Quetzalcoatl. One in particular was thousands of years old.

When the Lord convicted him to destroy the idols, he was thunderstruck. How could he obliterate valuable antiquities — the survivors of a long-gone culture? He considered, instead, donating the anthropological treasures to a museum.

Then, he realized that if the images had God's curses on them, he had no business bringing such a curse upon his favorite museum! So, with a hammer, he prayerfully turned the idols into gravel. And he was filled with great joy as he did it!

HOW ABOUT BOOKS AND RECORDS with satanic symbols on or in them? *Burn them!* The American Civil Liberties Union will have a fit at the very thought of book-burning, but you are completely within your rights to destroy your own books that teach another way than Jesus Christ.

Don't sell them to a second-hand bookstore, either.

Destroy them. *Burn them.* You don't even want your poor garbage man to dig a Satanic Bible out of your trash and get caught up in its lies!

What if destroying your teenager's beloved heavy-metal music collection breeds terrible rebellion in the child? What if your daughter is absolutely petrified at the idea of not being allowed to play *Dungeons and Dragons* with her friends?

Take authority!

You are the parent. The child is your responsibility.

Explain to the child what must be done. Pray with them — daily! Show them why action is vital. And if they refuse to cooperate, take matters into your own hands.

Get the evil materials out of your home.

IF YOUR ACTION BREEDS REBELLION, then go out of your way to spend time with your youngster. Is his or her soul worth your missing a promotion at work? Is his or her salvation worth your losing a big business deal?

Take a week off with your rebellious child — and nobody else. For seven days, sit on the beach or the fishing dock or hike the Grand Canyon or canoe down a scenic river as you listen to what your beloved child believes and thinks about life and Jesus Christ.

You may be shocked. But you'll have somewhere to start. You'll know what to pray about. And you'll show your child that you really care.

Begin a daily private time with your child. It might be 30 minutes at bedtime. Or 15 minutes in the sauna at the health club with your son before school. Or a daily bike ride to school with your youngster. But talk with your child. Pray with them, privately. Share with them spiritual truths that you are discovering in your daily walk. Talk about answered prayers.

Discuss whether their friends are going to be in heaven with them — and what needs to be done if not. Pray *for* your child when you are alone, too. Pray for your child with your spouse.

Sure, you may have to alter your schedule. Saving a soul may be time-consuming. *But, is your child worth it?*

Of course. I cannot imagine a worse heartbreak than dying — *even though I would know that I am about to get to walk heaven's streets of gold* — with the horrible knowledge that any of my four beautiful daughters might not join me after they have lived their lives.

Fortunately, I am quite assured that they will be!

HERE ARE SOME HINTS for Christian parents trying to protect their children from evil seductions of the dark side:

1. KNOW WHAT IS HAPPENING. A few years ago young people faced the danger of tremendous increase in exploitation from drugs. That threat will be with us for a long time, but a far greater threat right now is the occult revival. In this book I've tried to point out some of the many dangers shaping up in this area.

My biggest fear is that you will finish this book and go on to something else without doing anything about the occult menace in your own home. It's not enough to read and agree with what I've said here.

Look at the books and magazines your children are reading. Know what's going on in the schools your children attend. An English teacher in New Jersey drew the shades in her classroom and put out the lights while she told the class of her psychic experience. "I think I'm a medium," she said as she told of the predictions she had made and the spirits she had contacted. In a psychology class in another school the students were given lessons in palm reading, pendulum divination and the like.

A high school in Minnesota has a course in the supernatural in which the students visit cemeteries, lie in coffins, watch cremations, and imagine what it is like to be dead. Hundreds of other schools and colleges today have official courses in witchcraft, magic, and various phases of occult study. And recently the federal government gave a grant to the International Meditation Society to train 100 high-school teachers to teach transcendental meditation, a form of Hinduism.

From the seventh to 12th grades, teens listen to 11,000 hours of music at the rate of four to six hours a day, according to some experts. That represents more time than they spend in school from first grade through high school graduation — and certainly more time than they will spend in Sunday school!

Heavy metal music is seducing youngsters into believing that death is the only way out of whatever situation they feel to be insurmountable. As a result, nationally, about 14 teens commit suicide every day in the United States. Not all the musicians believe in the occult. They're just in the business of selling records — and currently this is one form that really sells. But their message is the same: drugs, sex, alcohol and the occult provide a powerful, desirable way of life.

Some groups, however, make no attempt to hide or even disguise their satanic interest. Motley Crue, for example, uses satanic symbols on their album jackets — as does Slayer. King Diamond's and Venom's albums are a virtual how-to course in performing demonic rituals, exploring such topics as necrophilia (sex with corpses), incest, rape, torture and human sacrifice.

Dave Hart, a research analyst who specializes in studying rock music for Menconi Ministries, says there are three types of heavy metal:

• Party metal, which concentrates on the joys of recreational sex and chemical abuse — typified by such groups as Bon Jovi, Motley Crue and Def Leppard;

• Thrash metal, which has a focus on violence and death, as performed by Mettalica, Megadeth and Anthrax; and

• Black metal, which is blatantly satanic, encouraging occult experimentation and guiding the listener in performing sacrilege, blood rites, blasphemy, black magic and demonic adoration, as typified by Lizzy Borden, King Diamond, Slayer and Venom.

2. KNOW THE TRUTH ABOUT THE OCCULT. The people pushing meditation claim it gets students off drugs and into better attitudes. What if it's the opening wedge for something worse than drugs? Remember, heroin was first marketed as a harmless painkiller — and was as available as aspirin.

I urge parents to read what the Bible says about the occult. I've already mentioned a number of passages on this subject. Here are some powerful ones: Deuteronomy 18:9-22; Ezekiel 13:17-23; Isaiah 8:19-20; 47:9-13; Galatians 5:19-25; 2 Corinthians 11:14,15; Revelation 22:15. Study them and talk with your kids about them.

3. WARN YOUR CHILDREN about the dangers of the occult. Debby Berman wrote in the *Hollywood Free Paper,* a Christian journal, of how she read a book about spiritualism during her junior year in high school. "I was fascinated," she said, "by the strange powers I'd acquired and thought that if I got deeper and deeper into the occult that I would finally discover what I was looking for."

Debby was assaulted mentally and physically by her spirit acquaintances; visible bruises appeared on her skin. One night she was attacked so furiously that she called on Jesus to help her. In the darkness of her room she saw Him drive away the demons and felt His victorious presence.

Pat Boone's young daughter Laury once joined some friends at school in chanting some witchcraft incantations. Although she did not take it seriously, Pat and Shirley Boone say their daughter's personality changed in a frightening way until she was delivered through prayer.

Your young people should know what can happen to them in the satanic world of the occult. But don't open their minds to the demonic by overstimulating them with occult horror stories. Give them a positive view of the supernatural world. Let them see how great God is, what a wonderful friend Jesus is, and how completely the Holy Spirit can guard anyone who lives in His power. Lead your children and young people to read the Bible for themselves and to absorb its balanced, spiritually healthful view of the invisible — as well as the visible — realm.

4. JOIN OTHERS OF LIKE MIND. Get together with other Christians to discuss the spiritual and mental well-being of your children. The schools and the public media may listen politely to what one or two parents say, but they aren't likely to do anything about it unless a group of individuals band together and show some collective muscle. If organizations of power and influence face the power of a united citizenry, they will listen and do something.

Your church or Bible-study group may be the natural place to begin such a group. In any case, remember that if your faith doesn't lead to Christian action, it is lifeless (James 2:17).

5. FIND OUT WHAT YOU CAN DO to stop the occult onslaught. You may need to protest. The federal government has ruled any form of Christian teaching or prayer out of the pulic schools. Every Christian parent should join a protest that will be heard clear to Congress and the Supreme Court whenever other religions, whether in the form of witchcraft, spiritualism, Eastern meditation, fortune telling, spiritualism or whatever, are brought into the schools. If God has to go out of the schools, let's not sit by idly while Satan marches in.

Or you may need to join other Christians in new legislation. Certainly if the Bible can no longer be read in school, other religions must not be promoted there. In any case, you can make your voice heard loud and clear by your school board and all those with power to influence your children's minds and hearts.

AS CHRISTIANS, MANY OF US don't like to get involved in politics. It's usually dirty and disillusioning. But we can remember this question: "Who knoweth whether thou art come to the kingdom for such a time as this?" (Esther 4:14). And we should by all means remember the Jewish boy who was carried into a distant land to be educated in a pagan court. The court was filled with magicians and astrologers who were believed to have all kinds of deep wisdom. The Jewish youth was supposed to learn all this, but he refused to forget his God or the Scriptures. When crisis came to the government, young Daniel knew the answers to the questions that baffled the astrologers and magicians. And in due course he rose to a position of great power and influence in that government, pagan as it was. Read the whole story in the Book of Daniel.

If we don't get involved for Christ's sake, we'll have to let everything go to the devil.

Who is most susceptible?

Teens are the most vulnerable, according to experts. However the term "teen" is deceptive these days. Children as young as 11 years are increasingly battered by peer pressures and the instability of puberty.

So, be careful if the following describes your 11-19-year-old:

• Intelligent, creative, curious
• An under- or over-achiever
• Involved in any sort of drug use or alcohol abuse
• Deeply devoted to heavy metal or punk rock music
• A victim of physical or emotional abuse
• Involved in role-playing games

WHAT IF YOU BEGIN TO SUSPECT that your child is secretly involved in satanism? Take immediate action.

According to police consultant Patricia Pulling, the largest obstacle to effective law enforcement in ritual and occult crime is denial.

"City officials, police department brass and the citizens don't want to admit this kind of activity is going on in their area," she says. "Or they attraibute it to kids playing harmless games. Believe me, it does go on, and it is not harmless. It's very real.

Pulling knows what she's talking about. The police detective became interested in the problems of fighting the occult when her 16-year-old son committed suicide as the result of a curse place on him by his dungeon-master while he was playing *Dungeons and Dragons*.

He'd become absorbed in the game at school where teachers in his accellerated classes for brighter students believed it was valuable in the development of logical thinking.

Pulling says that the truly dangerous form of the game is not the board version available in toy stores. That's just an introduction into the deeper horror. The game becomes intense when players learn to play it entirely in their minds as they respond to various situations created by the game's leader, called the dungeon-master.

Players responses are determined by their assumed characters, which may range from apprentice thief to master wizard-warrior. The object of the game is to stay alive, and "whatever it takes" is the key to survival.

PARENTS WOULD BE WISE to make the same distinction that police take between serious satanist criminals and "dabblers."

Dabblers are those just experimenting.

Yes, their playing with evil is dangerous. But how fortunate when a parent finds that a child is dabbling — before he or she gets caught up in the dark swirl of demonic power.

When ritual crime is suspected, Det. Pulling, recommends that investigating officers include the following list on their formal, court-ordered search warrant. It's a valuable list for parents, too, who are concerned that their child is playing with darkness. Remember, of course, that wisdom must be used in evaluating the evidence found in a search of your child's possessions.

Here's Detective Pulling's *Search Warrant Checklist:*

• Occult games (I Ching, *ouija* boards, tarot cards, crystal ball, fantasy role-playing games such as *Dungeons and Dragons*)

- Ashes from fire pits, including fireplaces and wood stoves.
- Robes and detachable hoods
- Gongs, drums and bells
- Wooden stand for an altar, a marble slab or crosses
- Chalice, goblet, cruet
- Phallus (sculpture of the male sex organ)
- Heavy wooden staff, sword, knives
- Small velvet pillow, scarlet in color
- Bullwhip, cat o'nine tails, ligatures
- Mirror
- Animal mask, possibly papier mache
- Black satin or velvet glove for the right hand
- Large ruby ring, worn on the first finger of the right hand
- Flash powder, smoke bombs
- Incense
- Body paint, face paint
- Metal crown with four candle holders
- Ferns, palms
- Human or animal bones (especially skull, long bones, finger bones)
- Coffin

• Ritual books, black books, diaries (such as the *Book of Shadows,* which may be handwritten)

- Medallions with satanic symbols
- Occult jewelry
- Small animals in cages
- Graph paper for fantasy games
- Oddly shaped dice

• Horror masks and costumes
• Crystals
• Small metal figurines of mythological nature
• Posters of mythological beings, animals, half-animals
• Nightmarish posters
• Sexual, particularly sado-masochistic, posters
• Posters of heavy metal and punk rock stars
• Paraphernalia related to the martial arts — such as ninja costumes and throwing stars

OBVIOUSLY, MANY NORMAL YOUNGSTERS will have one or two of some of these items. However, the wise parent will examine the situation carefully if the child seems to be accumlating quite a few items on the list — particularly if the youngster is secretive about it, has begun disappearing for unexplained passages of time, and begins refusing to have anything to do with the worship and sacraments of Jesus Christ.

But, you may ask, what is the harm in an inquisitive teen "dabbling" in some of this stuff? Read carefully the next two chapters, which describe what happened to friends of mine who saw no danger in "dabbling" — just for fun.

21

MR. RIVERS, THE DECEIVING DEMON

Michael and his wife

took me on a fantastic evening out in Los Angeles. Over a great steak dinner, these two faithful Christians began to tell me of a personal nightmare — which demonstrates just why God's children are not even supposed to *dabble* in the dark arts.

"Nicky, we've been through some things we've hardly dared tell anyone about," declared Constance. "Most people would think we were off our rockers!"

The whole thing began, they told me, when they moved into a house in Encino, one of those architectural works of art you often see in California, especially in or near Hollywood — a 90-percent-glass, twenty-two-room mansion set on an estate of lush gardens, tropical trees, and flowers of every kind and color. Yet, when it is very foggy or stormy outside, you get a very eerie, strange feeling.

RIGHT AFTER THEY MOVED IN, Constance sensed something horrible about the house: *An evil presence she grew to call "Mr. Rivers."*

"At first," Michael said with a grin, "when she began telling me about Mr. Rivers I wondered if she ought to see a psychiatrist!" He shook his head. "Even after seeing it with my own eyes, it's still hard to believe."

Michael had just left the house one morning when Constance's brother, George, who was staying with them, came into the kitchen looking shaken. After he had gulped down a cup of coffee, he burst out, "This is the funniest place I've ever been in."

"What do you mean, George?" asked Constance.

"When I woke up this morning I felt like I was suffocating. There was a pillow over my head and it seemed like someone was pushing it down onto my face. I couldn't breathe! At first I thought it was some practical joker."

When George paused, Constance asked, "Well, what was it? Don't keep me in suspense!"

"That's just it," said George with a worried frown. "I managed to push the pillow away — and no one was there!"

Constance said, "You've got to be kidding."

But he wasn't.

Soon afterward Michael's niece, Tiny, who was also staying there at the time, told Constance she had often felt that someone was in her room at night. "Several times my door opened and closed just like someone was coming into the room," Tiny said, "but no one was there. I was scared to tell anyone because I thought you'd all laugh at me."

ONE NIGHT, MICHAEL SAID, the front door opened and closed while the family was in the living room, just as if an invisible man had come in. Another night Michael and Constance were getting ready for bed when Constance rolled down the covers of their circular bed, which is usually topped with TV pillows.

Constance put the TV pillow on her side of the bed on the floor while Michael was brushing his teeth in the bathroom. When little Michael, Jr., who hates bedtime, called Constance, she went to his room to tuck him in. Returning, she found her TV pillow back on the bed.

"Michael!" Constance called as her husband came back from the bathroom. "What's going on here?"

When Constance pointed out that her pillow had mysteriously popped back on the bed, Michael was baffled.

That night Constance lay awake for a long time while everyone else in the house slept. As she mulled over the strange recent events, the thought came to her mind: *There is a spirit in this house and he is revealing himself.*

"Why, that's ridiculous," thought Constance. But the idea would not go away.

In the middle of the night, when everyone else was asleep, Constance heard the clatter of pots and pans. In the morning the kitchen was a bizarre sight. A heavy frying pan was in the middle of the floor. A large pressure cooker lay on its side behind the refrigerator, the coffee pot was in the sink, and knives and forks were scattered in odd corners of the kitchen.

"What was going on here last night?" Bea, the housekeeper, asked Constance.

"THAT'S WHAT I'D LIKE TO KNOW," retorted Constance as she helped Bea put the things where they belonged. When Michael came in he refused to believe the girls' story. "All this is getting to be just too much," he said.

The Peterson's home had once been owned by a well-to-do gentleman named Rivers. Neighbors told Constance and Michael that Mr. Rivers used to love to lie in the round sunken tub in the bathroom and enjoy the sunshine that pours through the wide glass doors. Mr. Rivers, now dead, had a attractive wife — not unlike Constance.

Desiring more privacy, Constance called in an interior decorator, John Warden, to put a curtain in front of the glass doors. He put up a massive curtain rod and came back the next day to hang the curtain. That morning, while Constance was tending the clothing shop which she and Michael own and manage, she got an excited telephone call from John Warden.

"Mrs. Peterson," asked Warden, "did someone break into your house last night?"

"Break into our house? Not as far as I know. Why?"

"That big curtain rod," said John Warden, "has been bent clear out of shape."

"You can't be serious!" exclaimed Constance.

He was. The rod, Michael and Constance discovered when they inspected it that night, had been bent into a circle. Constance said, "It's been bent back to where they say Mr. Rivers's drapes used to be."

She and Michael remembered several other changes they had made in the house — all of which had been mysteriously resisted.

Constance declared: "This has got to stop." She raised her voice. "Mr. Rivers, that new curtain rod is going to stay where we put it. I want you to quit this nonsense."

NOW LET ME TELL YOU SOMETHING about these dear friends of mine. Constance, like many other Californians, had been worried over the widespread predictions that an earthquake was about to shake the State of

California into the ocean. So she confided these fears to an *astrologer* friend. *An astrologer!*

Well, I don't believe that you and I are permitted to remain in close fellowship with people who have given themselves over to evil forces of darkness. We're supposed to share our faith with them. If they refuse to believe, then we are to leave them alone — particularly people who are committing such sin as astrology, palmistry or spiritualism.

Nevertheless, Constance listened to her friend, who advised her: *"Constance, you are the type of person who attracts spirits. Don't ever light candles — they draw spirits to someone like you."*

Well, do they? Or did such a warning merely plant a seed in Constance's mind? A silly superstition? A fear of something Christians need not fear?

Is Constance the *sort of person* who attracts spirits?

No! I do believe that Lucifer used a servant of his, a seemingly well-meaning astrologer, to plant this tempting seed of interest in Constance's mind: *Am I the sort of person who attracts spirits? How interesting! What kind of spirits? What will they do?*

THE "WARNING" WAS JUST A CLEVER LURE. And Satan, who desires all of us to become fascinated with and fearful of his evil — rather than at peace in God's might and love — dangled the pretty bait.

This seducing "warning" became a toehold for a tormenting demon sent to pretend to be the deceased Mr. Rivers.

Why would Satan bother?

Well, just look at where this episode took Constance. Naively, this fine Christian took the bait and turned not to Jesus for protection from this irritating demonic visitor — but instead to the forbidden! She found herself attempting to contact a ghost, a spirit — *the dead Mr. Rivers.*

One night in their bedroom, Michael had put on some romantic music and Constance had turned out all the lights and lit some beautiful candles they had received as a gift.

The entire room was aglow in the hazy candlelight. Michael turned to Constance and saw that suddenly her face had become panic-stricken. She had a desperate look in her eyes. She began gasping for air and trying to scream but could only whisper, "I feel like I'm having a heart attack. Help me! Help me!"

She felt as if she was being smothered. She tried to keep calm, but it was too much.

"What's happening?" Michael frantically exclaimed. He became panicky. "What do you want me to do — call an ambulance? Let me help you!"

BUT CONSTANCE, DESPERATELY TRYING TO YELL, said in a hoarse voice, "Don't touch me! Blow out the candles!"

She kept repeating, "Blow out the candles!" as she crawled to the end of the bed and yanked open the curtains. Then she slipped off the bed and literally crawled on her hands and knees across the bedroom floor out to the patio. As Michael extinguished all the candles, Constance's breathing started to return to normal.

Can't you see Satan at work?

Just imagine the fear now embedded in Constance's mind. Recovering somewhat, she got up and slowly walked over to the edge of the patio overlooking the city below. Still in a daze, she peered out into the darkness and the city lights. As she stood there, shaken from the traumatic experience, she remembered how she had felt — that her life seemingly being drawn away and she was being taken to a horrible place from which she would never return.

She had felt perfectly fine before the "attack" and hadn't had any recent illnesses, and yet suddenly, with no warning, she couldn't breathe. As the cool night breezes blew against her body and hair, questions began to flow through her mind. "Why?" Why, Michael?" Constance asked over and over.

She had to have an answer.

One evening Constance came home and found George, Fern (a good friend of the family), and several of George's friends in the living room playing with a *ouija* board. She didn't know much about this so-called game and although she is a Christian, she wasn't aware of its evil power.

"Constance," urged George, "come and sit down with us and ask some questions. Talk to Mr. Rivers on the *ouija* board."

Constance thought of the bizarre experiences she had had in the past. "But the *ouija* is just a game," she said.

"No, it isn't," said George. "It's surprising what you can find out sometimes from a *ouija* board."

Let me repeat: *ouija is a very dangerous game.* No one should have anything to do with it, as Constance and George now know.

Stay away from *Ouija!*

Since you may not know just how dangerous *ouija* boards are, let's pause for a moment and consider the findings of occult expert Edmund Gruss, quoted in *Handbook of Today's Religions* by Josh McDowell and Don Stewart:

"The ouija board should be seen as a device which sometimes actually makes contact with the supernatural.

"The many cases of 'possession' after a period of ouija board use support the claim that supernatural contact is made through the board. Psychics and parapsychologists have received letters from hundreds of people who have experienced 'possession' (an invasion of their personalities). Rev. Donald Page, a well-known clairvoyant and exorcist of the Christian Spiritualist Church, is reported as saying that most of his 'possession' cases 'are people who have used the ouija board," and that "this is one of the easiest and quickest ways to become possessed. While Page views these 'possessions' as caused by disincarnate entities, the reality of possession is still clear. The Christian sees the invader as an evil spirit (demon.)

"The board has been subjected to tests which support supernatural intervention. The testing of the board was presented in an article by Sir William Barrett, in the September 1914 Proceedings of the American Society for Psychical Research. The Barrett report indicated that the board worked efficiently with the operators blindfolded, the board's alphabet rearraged and its surface hidden from the sight of those working it. It worked with such speed and accuracy under those tests that Barrett concluded:

"'Reviewing the results as a whole, I am convinced of their supernormal character, and that we have here an exhibition of some intelligent, disincarnate agency, mingling with the personality of one or more of the sitters and guiding their muscular movements.'"

In short, it's evil.

It's cursed.

It's forbidden.

Stay away!

CONSTANCE SAT DOWN WITH THE REST of the group around the board and started questioning it. As you may know, *ouija* operates when those present rest their fingers very lightly on a plastic disk which answers questions by moving to various points of the board. A typical *ouija* board contains all the letters of the alphabet, the numerals, and the words YES, NO, and GOODBYE.

"Do you know my children?" asked Constance.

The disk spelled out their initials.

Constance continued questioning: "Are you jealous?"

YES

"Who are you jealous of?"

As Constance watched the board spell M-I-K-E, she remembered the number of times Michael had said he had telephoned her and no one had answered. After several of these incidents, someone discovered the telephone volume had been moved to the lowest point. She asked the *ouija* board, "Did you turn the phone down?"

YES

"Are you jealous of men in my house?"

YES

Constance began to be frightened because she realized this "game" was no joke. More afraid than ever of whatever it was that apparently had a jealous spirit and destructive, murderous intentions, Constance fell to her knees and began praying: "O God, I don't want to be possessed by any spirit but Your Spirit. Please help me. Amen."

Immediately the disk shot to the word GOODBYE and then shot right off the board, bouncing onto the floor.

AS SOON AS I HEARD about "Mr. Rivers" I spent much time in prayer with Michael and Constance.

"You know," I said one night when I was at their house, "it just isn't possible for a person's spirit to float around on earth after death. Jesus promised the thief who repented on the cross next to His, 'This day shalt thou be with me in paradise.' After the rich man in Jesus' parable died, he begged permission to go back to earth to warn his brothers not to follow him to hell, but it was not permitted for him to cross the gulf.

"I don't doubt you've been troubled by a spirit, but I cannot believe it is Mr. Rivers's. The devil is a liar and deceiver, you know. It looks to me as if you've been disturbed by a spirit entity that's been trying to confuse you. All the evidence shows that evil spirits have many of the characteristics of psychotics.

"They are deceptive, unpredictable, sometimes irrationally destructive. Some of the things that happened here Satan may have engineered simply to draw you away from Christ. How he would love to have you believe in a spirit world instead of heaven and hell! How he would love to have you believe in him instead of Christ!"

Michael and Constance asked me to pray that the spirit world depart. So we all joined together as I prayed:

"LORD, FILL THIS HOUSE from top to bottom with Your love and grace. May Michael and Constance and all that dwell here look only to You for help and guidance. Fill them all with Your Spirit, and deliver them from every kind of evil. Let the blood of Jesus keep them safe forever. Amen."

"You know, Nicky," said Constance, "ever since you prayed for us that night, we haven't heard from 'Mr. Rivers.' Our house is covered by the blood of Jesus Christ and nothing can harm us."

Why did I tell you

that story? I believe you need to know how Satan works, *how* he deceives us — and all the marvelous tools Almighty God gives us to *win*.

For example, Philippians 4:8 is full of guidance as we venture into the evil underworld:

"... Fix your thoughts on what is true and good and right. Think about things that are pure and lovely, and dwell on the fine, good things in others. Think about all you can praise God for and be glad about." (Living Bible)

What does this mean? Some might think that it is a caution for us not to read a book like this — that we should stay away from ugly, depressing stuff that will drag us down. But the Bible is so full of commands for us to march into battle — and assurances that our opponent is the defeated weakling that he really is!

So, I believe the verse means for us to be positive about the fight we face! Don't dwell on frightening, ugly things that will stir up fear in your heart or fill your mind with doubt!

Instead, focus on the fact that our Lord can and will protect you against any evil.

Just look at the verses that preceed:

"Always be full of joy in the Lord; I say it again, rejoice! Let everyone see that you are unselfish and considerate in all you do. Remember that the Lord is coming soon. Don't worry about anything; instead, pray about everything; tell God your needs and don't forget to thank him for his answers. If you do this you will experience God's peace, which is far

more wonderful than the human mind can understand. His peace will keep your thoughts and your hearts quiet and at rest as you trust in Christ Jesus."

Praise God for these promises!

IF WE OBEY THEM, WE AREN'T GOING to find ourselves enticed by the exciting stories in this book about Satan. We aren't going to dabble in a little occult experimentation of our own in palm readers' evil lairs, "checking them out" to see just how awful they are.

Instead, filled with the peace that passes understanding — which comes only from God — *we will be ready to fight!*

And we have such *mighty weapons!* Do you realize that we are given authority to lock Satan up? If you think that sounds ridiculous, read Matthew 16:19: "And I will give you the keys of the Kingdom of Heaven; whatever doors you lock on earth shall be locked in heaven ..."

Perhaps you'd rather check that out in the traditional *King James Version:* "And I will give unto thee the keys of the kingdom of heaven; and whatsoever thou shalt bind on earth shall be bound in heaven ..."

This verse gives us the authority to tell Satan to stop dead in his tracks. We have jurisdiction — from Almighty God — to halt Satan. Then, you have the right to tell him to leave.

To go.

To leave the scene.

READ LUKE 10:19 IF YOU DOUBT THAT: "And I give you authority over all the power of the Enemy ... nothing shall injure you."

Hang onto that important truth, my friend. Quote it at the devil. Tell him that you have authority over his power — and that he has to leave you alone!

Here is some more ammunition:

Mark 16:17: And these signs shall follow them that believe; in my name shall they cast out devils ..."

Revelation 12:11: And they overcame him [Satan] by the blood of the Lamb, and by the word of their testimony ..."

James 4:7: Submit yourselves therefore to God. Resist the devil, and he will flee from you ...

Matthew 7:7-8: Ask, and you will be given what you ask for. Seek, and you will find. Knock, and the door will be opened. For everyone who asks, receives. Anyone who seeks, finds. If only you will knock, the door will be opened.

Matthew 21:22: You can get anything — *anything* you ask for in prayer — if you believe.

Matthew 18: 19: I also tell you this — if two of you agree down here on earth concerning anything you ask for, my Father in heaven will do it for you.

Mark 11:24: Listen to me! You can pray for anything, and if you believe, you have it; it's yours.

And you can look up these: *John 14:13; John 15:7; John 16:23; Hebrews 4:16; Psalm 37:4; Psalm 91: 15; Psalm 145:18-19; Jeremiah 33:3; I John 3:22; Romans 8:31; Mark 9:23; Jeremiah 32:27.* All are excellent! *All are effective when you need to tell Satan just where he stands.*

22

A LITTLE BOY'S SEDUCTION

Demons glitter and fascinate,

but they don't want you to know what they are really up to. So they use all sorts of tricks and disguises.

Why? *Because they are scared.*

That's the absolute truth.

These invisible spirits don't like to be exposed. Most of the time they do very well not letting anyone know they are around. But when Jesus came to Earth as a man, the veil was drawn back and they could be seen in His great light, trying to organize people against Him, lurking in an evil heart here, a deranged mind there.

The demons knew Jesus and trembled at His power.

Today, as the time draws closer when He will come back, once more the evil spirits seem to be exposing themselves. They will stop at nothing to try to get whoever they can under their power.

And one of their favorite tools is deception. They pretend to be friendly and helpful.

FROM HIS EARLIEST YEARS MIGUEL, a boy in the Dominican Republic, had been exposed to the witchcraft that you find in so much of in the countries of the Caribbean.

(Perhaps I should explain why I do not give Miguel's last name. To

protect his privacy, I am using another first name and describing him differently just a bit to disguise him. I have done the same with Olga and a few others — for if you were to share your personal testimony with me in private, and were ashamed of some of the things you once did, I would honor your request to write about you using a different name and saying you are from Los Angeles when you might really live in Atlanta!)

AS A LITTLE BOY, ONE NIGHT "Miguel" found a blue bottle under a banana tree on his father's plantation. He knew it had been put there to work a curse on his father's bananas and destroy his crops, so he threw the bottle over the fence that surrounded the banana grove. As he ran toward home he saw red eyes glaring at him from the shadows.

One night when Miguel was six years old he felt someone in his room where he still slept in an old-fashioned trundle bed. At first Miguel thought his mother had come into the room. Then he became conscious of a light in the room and of someone standing by his bed. He felt as though this person was smiling at him. Finally the light faded and the presence seemed to go away.

"Mama," Miguel called to his mother across the hall, "were you in here?"

Miguel's mother came quickly to the door. "No, son," she said. "Why do you ask?"

"Oh, I thought someone was in here," said the little boy. "It seemed like someone came in and looked at me."

"It must have been an angel," Miguel's mother told him.

When Miguel was eight he was visited again. This time — and frequently afterward — several persons seemed to come to him at odd times. Each time the boy felt that he was among friends.

MIGUEL WAS A LONELY BOY. The youngest of three sons, he longed to play with his brothers, but with the cruelty children often practice unconsciously, they usually left little brother out of their activities. Who wanted to be bothered looking after the baby of the family?

As a result, Miguel often played alone. He started looking in a mirror, imagining the person he saw was another self, talking with his imaginary alter ego. Sometimes the other self took on a strange unexpected reality.

When Miguel started playing with a *ouija* board, the "friends" and the imaginary self began delivering strange messages. Miguel found himself communicating with beings who lured him into exciting experiments.

He found that he could summon what appeared to be invisible but powerful spirits. They made uncanny predictions and seemed to guard him from danger.

FOUR OF MIGUEL'S SCHOOL FRIENDS MADE PLANS to pick him up for a drive to Santo Domingo. When they arrived at his home in a car, they were stupefied at his sudden refusal to go with them. *"I just don't feel like it,"* was his only explanation. As they drove angrily away without him, Miguel thought to himself: *How can I tell them? Would they believe me if I told them that my spirit friends warned me not to go?*

The next day Miguel was not surprised when the news came that all four friends were in the hospital. As they had neared Santo Domingo, a truck coming around a curve on their side of the road sideswiped their car and sent it off the road into a fence.

Miguel went deeper and deeper into witchcraft.

One day he invoked a spirit that came to him by the name of Mephistopheles. Promising him unusual powers, Mephistopheles suggested that Miguel perform strange tasks that led him ever farther into a demonic world. Soon Miguel dipped into astrology and became fascinated at how his life seemed to have been shaped by the conjunction of the planets at his birth.

At a Florida university he added to the subjects he was taking a course in astrological psychology. Miguel also studied Buddhism. Buddha's doctrines of seeking unity with the divine through meditation strongly appealed to him. He was especially impressed that Buddha was teaching this hundreds of years before Jesus was born.

It all added up to a neat, attractive package: *guidance, protection from danger, at-one-ness with the Infinite.*

THEN MIGUEL MET ANNIE. She listened carefully to everything Miguel told her so enthusiastically about his adventures in witchcraft. Then she told him what Jesus Christ had done for her. She knew something about spirits, she said. She herself had often been obsessed with a feeling of depression and despondency, and she had been led on occasion to command an evil spirit to leave a person, in the name of Jesus.

"But these aren't evil spirits," Miguel protested hotly. "Through Buddhism I'm close to God."

"Jesus is the only way to God," said Annie. "There is no other way.

He said, 'I am the way, the truth, and the life: no man cometh unto the Father, but by me'" (John 14:6).

Miguel seethed when Annie talked like that about Christ. He felt that she was putting down the whole beautiful world he had discovered. The name of *Jesus* especially angered him. But something about this girl kept him talking to her. When she told him very calmly that she was simply letting God speak through her, Miguel knew deep in his heart that she was speaking the truth. Her words burned into his consciousness with great conviction.

Then, spirits began bothering him at night. Sometimes he would hear dogs barking nearby as he felt their presence. He told Annie, "I've told the spirits to go away and not come back."

"They will come back," said Annie. "And soon you will begin to see how they were never your friends like you thought."

And then the battle began.

Annie awoke in her dormitory room about 3 A.M. Strange noises sounded throughout the dormitory — noises she had never heard before, for it was usually very quiet in the dorm at night.

Annie was aware of a wicked presence nearby. Fear gripped her for several nights as the same sequence was repeated.

Then, she put her Bible study to work — charging into spiritual battle.

FIRST, SHE REMEMBERED PHILIPPIANS 2:9 — which proclaims that the Name of Jesus is the Name above every name. Then, she remembered guidelines we are given in Jude 1:9. There, the great Archangel Michael did not insult Satan or even accuse Satan, but just spoke the words: "The Lord rebuke you"

And so, in the Name of Jesus, she rebuked the devil from frightening her or harrassing her.

Interestingly enough, the noise outside halted.

Instantly.

When she found herself still a bit scared, listening in the silence for it to come back, she remembered Jude 1:20.

"But you, dear friends, must build up your lives ever more strongly upon the foundation of our holy faith, learning to pray in the power and strength of the Holy Spirit."

AND SHE WENT ON THE ATTACK, DECLARING: "Father God, I ask the protection that You have promised! You are Lord! You are God! You have given me power over the evil ones, so in obedience, I declare: 'In the Name of Jesus, I rebuke you, Satan! I bind you! You cannot stop me!'
"

And the boldness of the Lord rose up in her as she began to remember all sorts of good Scriptures, such as 2 Corinthians 4:3 and 4:

If the Good News we preach is hidden to anyone, it is hidden from the one who is on the road to eternal death. Satan, who is the god of this evil world, has made him blind, unable to see the glorious light of the Gospel that is shining upon him, or to understand the amazing message we preach about the glory of Christ, who is God.

Yes! Immediately, she understood why Miguel had such trouble hearing the Gospel. But she rejoiced that he was still so interested — even hungry for the truth.

And she felt stronger and stronger.

ONE EVENING AS ANNIE AGAIN TALKED with Miguel, she became aware of an alien spirit presence. The apartment door suddenly slammed shut. Miguel seemed nervous but tried to cover it by talking, jumping from one topic to another. He knew that a spirit had entered the room and hoped Annie wouldn't notice it.

Annie sensed the presence but this time she felt no fear. Instead, although she felt weak within herself, she sought help from God and felt powerful rushes of strength from His Spirit. To each of Miguel's arguments against Christ's claims she found an answer.

The dark, heavy presence seemed to grow. A curtain over the window billowed out — although the window was shut. A little later the cover of Miguel's record player popped open.

Miguel said, "There is a spirit in the room."

"I know," said Annie.

"Start praying," Miguel asked.

ANNIE SAID A SIMPLE PRAYER: In the name of Jesus she told the spirit to leave — *and she felt it go.*

Soon afterward Miguel knelt down and renounced the spirits with whom he had dealt for so long. Annie, praising God, told him of Jesus' parable of the spirit who left a man, only to return to the empty place later with seven more evil spirits.

"The way to keep that from happening," she said, "is to be filled with the Holy Spirit."

And so, to her immense joy, he knelt with her. He gave his life to Jesus Christ and asked the Holy Spirit to fill his life. He rose up filled with the joy of His salvation.

BUT NOW THAT HE'D MADE A CLEAN commitment, Miguel found he had lost something. His powers of witchcraft were gone, along with the demonic guidance and protection he had grown used to.

But the evil ones had not forgotten him. One morning about six weeks later Miguel was feeling proud of his Christian growth as he rode his bicycle through the little college town. As he came to a stop sign at an intersection, his hands and feet froze. He could not stop. He shot at about 25 miles an hour into the main thoroughfare.

There was only one car on the street, but it was headed directly for Miguel.

"God, help me!" Miguel silently pleaded, aware of his helplessness. Somehow — no one can explain how — there was no collision. So Miguel learned about the new kind of protection and guidance of the Holy Spirit. And then he learned how to attack.

WHY BOTHER, YOU MAY ASK? Why tackle the evil that wants to seduce our kids and influence our civilization?

Well, let's look at three societies today where demonic forces run rampant!

23

SOCIETIES WHERE EVIL SPIRITS RULE!

Come with me

and we'll visit the modern-day nations of Thailand, Zimbabwe and Guatemala— real countries.

These are true accounts of real events.

They happened recently to real people.

Don't be so sure it can't happen here.

IN A RECENT ISSUE OF *GEO* MAGAZINE, travel writer Stanley Karnow tells of the challenges he encountered trying to do everyday business in Thailand — a kingdom in southeast Asia once called Siam.

"Moonlight flickered through the jungle foliage as three Buddhist monks, their orange robes rustling in the gentle breeze, encircled a white-gowned man sitting cross-legged within a square outlined by sacred thread.

"The smell of incense mingled with the acrid odor of burning candles. One monk chanted prayers while the other two placed offerings of chickens, ducks and green coconuts on a flimsy altar.

"Then, as the chant grew louder, the white-gowned man flung flaming foils of gold and silver to the heavens, and a sudden gust of wind whipped the forest clearing in apparent response to the incantation.

"THE WHITE-GOWNED FIGURE IN THAT RITUAL, performed one night not long ago on a hilltop in northern Thailand, was my friend

Udom Yenrudi, a Bangkok businessman. I had returned to Thailand to see him because we are partners in a mining company that has been going bankrupt.

"The trouble, Udom had learned from assorted seers and soothsayers, is that our mines, located in southern Thailand, are plagued by demons. He had arranged the ceremony in hopes of exorcising the sites, and though the purification process could take years, he assured me that we can now at least look forward to eventual solvency.

"'Do you really think it will work?' I asked him.

"'Well, if nothing more,' Udom replied, "it may improve our credit rating.'"

WHILE IT WOULD SEEM THAT WALL STREET might sneer at this sort of behavior, it should be emphasised that the author was "in Thailand, where the supernatural is natural."

"The Thai," he wrote, "are obsessed with astrology, palmistry, phrenology, telepathy, mystical charms, talismans, magic herbs, roots and potions ..." and by ever-present good and evil spirits.

The author noted that every private home and public building in Thailand contains shrines to demon spirits — who they believe require daily handouts of food and flowers as the price for blessing the faithful.

Astrology rules everything. In fact, he said, the king and his court "will not budge without checking the sun and the stars in advance.

"Merchants open new shops only at auspicious hours, and no peasant would think of either planting or harvesting his crops before placating the local gods."

Defendants in murder trials have been known to plead innocent on the grounds that evil spirits pulled the trigger.

"UDOM IS A SOPHISTICATED GENTLEMAN," wrote Karnow, "educated in England, who mingles familiarly with New York executives.

"But he also believes in sprites and fairies and the influence of witches. Thai perceive no conflict between orthodox religion and superstition ... they will count on a faith healer to cure a headache and at the same time consult a Buddhist monk for guidance on reincarnation — all without fear of being censured for heresy."

The Thai attribute wondrous authority to amulets that supposedly ensure affluence, strength, happiness and other good things, wrote the author. These may contain tiny images of various gods, mystical mottoes or pieces of animal bone, skin or tusk.

"A particularly ghoulish amulet favored by the Thai is the *luk krok*, a pendant containing a bit of human fetus, whose spirit purportedly endows its owner with incredible powers.

"One of Thailand's foremost army officers, Major General Sutsai Hasdin, is said to owe his extraordinary prowess to such a fetish, fashioned from the embryo of his stillborn twin brother.

"Many Thai families also preserve the pickled remains of unborn babies in the hollow statue of a child, the ghost serving as protector of the household."

KARNOW DESCRIBED JUST HOW he and his partner got into the mining business. In 1961, they visited a monk at a remote shrine and asked for spiritual guidance. The monk examined Udom's right palm and asked the date and hour of his birth.

"Then the monk reached into his robe, brought out a gold fountain pen and jotted down a few numbers, evidently doing some rapid astral accounting. Minutes later, he gazed at Udom and intoned: 'You will find wealth under the ground.'"

The author told how his partner was stunned. He'd been skeptical of an opportunity to buy an antimony mine in southern Thailand, down by the Malaysian border. However, "Udom's qualms about the project were now dispelled; destiny had clearly intervened ..."

Elaborate preparations to build proper shrines on the property, please the local spirits and conjure up ghosts that would protect the mine, however, were apparently ineffective. The mine was plagued with problems — not the least of which was no profits.

COME WITH ME TO ZIMBABWE — in the middle of Africa. Here our source is Credo Mutwa, author of *Indaba, My Children,* writing of his years as a witchdoctor. Here he describes the practice of giving herbs to a patient and causing the appearance of death. Then the night after the funeral, the wizard recovers the body, restoring the victim to semi-consciousness with drugs and magic for a special use — a real-live "zombie," called a *tokoloshe*.

According to the author:

"Cases are known to me where wizards have arranged the faked death of a particular person whom they had selected for a prospective zombie. The person is actually buried, but exhumed the same night and revived. He is then turned into a zombie and many days or weeks later, heavily decorated with the parts of other people's bodies also exhumed from graves, the puppet is induced to pay a particular victim an unexpected visit.

"The victim simply dies of fright. Any chance witness will relate a beautiful tokoloshe story to the police, and the police will dismiss it as so much nonsense."

Mutwa goes on to write that he knew witchdoctors who would raise mentally retarded infants as *tokoloshes*. He even claims he knew of a secret *tokoloshe* farm in recent years in the nearby country of Lesotho:

"With the arrival of the white man and Christianity, the killing of children who were born cretins and idiots went out of fashion, and these grotesque specimens of humanity grew plentiful. But an idiot is something no one misses should it mysteriously disappear — the parents least of all — and many of these idiots, particularly female, landed up in the hands of these wizards. They reared them, and when adult they mated with them and kept them in dark caves for their children to be born. Often in Lesotho — the land of ritual murder — the babies were brought into this world the caesarian way with no concern over the life of the mother. Parts of her body were used for medicines that were administered to her own baby to make it grow up in an atmosphere of deep evil …"

Mutwa writes in his book that the child was often surgically abused to make its back and limbs look deformed. Its tongue was carefully mangled to destroy any ability to speak. The little slave was taught to worship its cruel master and obey his every command.

What a horror story!

GUATEMALA IS THE "LAND OF ETERNAL SPRING," say the tourism posters. But up in its Sangre de Christo mountains in Central America, just across Mexico's southern border, an evil drama was enacted recently. A small, proud tribe of Quiche Indians, the Tzutujils, live on a narrow inlet on the high mountains' Lake Atitlan, nestled between three volcanos, Toliman, Atitlan and T'chuc. They believe they are protected by a local demon, an evil entity called Maximon.

Visitors are warned that he walks the streets at night, selecting victims to trick. He's an evil prankster and loves to pretend to be a crying baby in the shadows. But if anyone attempts to help the screaming infant, he turns into a vicious wild dog, ripping out the Good Samaritan's throat.

Other times, Maximon pretends to be a fisherman in trouble. When rescuers respond, he laughs and churns the lake with 10-foot waves, capsizing their dugout canoes and drowning all. To protect themselves, Tzutujil children sent on errands at night carry lit cigars to offer to the demon, should they encounter him.

IN THE 1950s, MISSIONARIES returned to the village for the first time in 200 years. They were stunned to find Maximon in such control. Inside the village's 500-year-old Catholic church, built on the ruins of a once-great Mayan pyramid-temple, Maximon sat enthroned in honor on what had been the altar. Over by the baptistry, a glass coffin displayed a statue of the dead Christ — unrisen from the dead.

Two priests decided to wrestle back the ancient church from the Mayan witch doctors. One night, they stole Maximon's idol and sold its carved head to a French archeologist. According to local belief, it is on display somewhere in Paris.

Villagers were furious. If you ask what happened to the priests, you'll be told one "joined the Underwater People" of the lake — ghostly spirits denied eternal rest because their drowned human bodies were never recovered. The other priest "became one of the Volcano People."

In fact, the two missionaries were dragged out of their hut by an angry mob. One was drowned in the middle of the lake. The other was hurled, live, into the bubbling caldera of San Pedro volcano. Two Indians who had befriended the priests were also killed, but two others were merely cursed for life.

TODAY THE TWO SURVIVING CONVERTS are still alive. One always has his arm or leg in a plaster cast and walks on crutches. His demonic curse was that he would always have a broken bone — for the rest of his life. The other's curse was that his children would be insane. He only has one son, who is completely incapacitated with mental disorders.

Inside the restored church, you'll find an uneasy truce. Visiting priests hold Mass. But the ornately carved altar has multiple panels of Maximon. A small chapel guards the front courtyard. Inside Maximon's image is on display during Holy Week — just before Easter.

But, all around the courtyard, there is bright and shining hope. All around town, there are study groups led by local Christians determined to take back this stronghold of demon worship.

They have seen true spiritual battle.

They know the power of evil.

But they know another mighty truth: Almighty God is not mocked. The name of Jesus Christ makes the demons flee.

They know that it is silly to fight the demonic with physical weapons — and without spiritual protection — that kidnapping venerated idols will just get you a watery grave with the Underwater People.

Running away isn't the answer, either. That's surrender to the ugly forces of darkness.

But armed with spiritual weapons — the Word of God and the many promises that we Christians have been given of victory over Satan — you can stand your ground and force the evil into retreat.

Here's how that works.

A GOOD FRIEND OF MINE WAS A VOLUNTEER lay-worker at the church there. He worked with the respected Father Stanley "Padre Francisco" Rother — who in 1982 was martyred in Guatemala's years-long civil war. It's an ongoing struggle between communist guerrilla bandits, the National Guard, local warlords, and the country's much-feared, shadowy death squads that assassinate anyone suspected of supporting or opposing the particular political figureheads of the day.

He tells of a personal encounter with Maximon — or perhaps a lesser demon.

"Late one night, I had to leave the rectory and go out into the back courtyard and into the laundry room to pick up our clothes. As I entered the laundry room, I was filled with sudden foreboding — bordering on utter panic."

An inner sense told him to flee — that something truly terrible was waiting in the unusually black shadows. A devout believer in Jesus Christ, the volunteer credits the Holy Spirit for giving him discernment of the evil.

"I WAS TREMBLING," HE TOLD ME, "but I rebuked the demon — which I could not see, but which I began to feel as a very cold, horrible presence. I declared into the evil blackness, 'In the name of Jesus Christ, the Messiah, the Son of Almighty God, I rebuke you! You cannot touch me! I belong to Him. Jesus is Lord!'"

Suddenly, the laundry room was not as dark or chilly. The evil was gone. Praising God, the volunteer returned to the rectory and told his story. A native deacon just grinned and shrugged.

"Sounds like you met Maximon," he chuckled.

"You mean he's *REAL?*"

"Sure," said the deacon. "You think people are scared of some stupid idol?"

IS THIS THE SORT OF AMERICA that those who are filling our land with demon-worship hope for? Fear of spirits? Faith in demons and vengeance and curses?

Yes.

Thank God for the liberating truth of Jesus Christ. We can put our hopes and trust in the hands of the One Master of the Universe who created everything and has pledged His eternal love for you and me.

Almighty God.

Not some angel of light proclaiming a false gospel.

Nor a demon pretending to be an astronaut from an "advanced" culture millions of years from Earth in another star system.

Like *E.T.: The Extraterrestrial.*

24

DECEPTION FROM 'OUTER SPACE'

"Nicky, how can you fear

nice little E.T., the poor marooned creature from outer space who loved little children and only wanted to phone home?"

You're surely familiar with the movie that made director Steven Spielberg even more millions of dollars than his blockbuster *Close Encounters of the Third Kind* on the same subject — contact between humans and thrilling, truth-giving aliens from far, far away.

I resent Spielberg's movies for several reasons. I resent one of his reoccuring humor techniques in which small child stars proclaim terrible obscenities while everybody in the theater laughs.

If you have not seen E.T., then you've been spared the "hilarious" scene in which 10-year-old actor Henry Thomas insults his big brother, calling him "penis breath."

I ALSO BELIEVE THAT SPIELBERG is being manipulated by evil forces that he cannot begin to understand to *condition* human minds to blindly accept some terrible things:

• That terrible ugliness is beautiful. I could write a whole book about this, but it's really nothing new. Satan desires to pervert beauty and majesty so that we will accept mediocre and lousy. I believe the artist Picasso was used in this same way. Just look at his effect on the world of art.

Suddenly, silly scrawls and misshapen hideousness was extremely "sophisticated" and expressive.

- That foul talk is *harmless* and cute. Just look at the above example. Children all across America are calling one another this nasty insult. And they're asking what it means. What a terrible thing for six-year-olds to be pondering how somebody gets "penis breath" and, since it's so funny, that maybe such an experiment might be harmless.

- That the loss of innocence is something to yearn for. Spielberg's movies tell our kids not only that they *already* know more than silly, stupid adults, but that they need to hurry their rush into sex and romance. Again, this very talented moviemaker is not the only offender. This great evil is everywhere in the entertainment world. There's a whole industry that cranks out teen movies on one deadly theme — *particularly when you consider the rampant spread of AIDS* — the excitement of the loss of virginity and the horror of being sexually inexperienced.

- That we need not look to the Creator for the answers of the universe. Instead, exciting little green men from the sky are going to come down and give us all the answers!

Let me state this for the record: I am very skeptical that there are *alien lifeforms* out there! Even if there are, we had better be enormously discerning as we listen to any "truth" they have for us — particularly about God.

What do I believe most of the "aliens" that fill supermarket tabloids and sensational TV specials really are?

Just demons masquerading!

Ah, Nicky, you may chuckle, why would they bother?

SATAN IS USING OUR FASCINATION IN UFOs just as he has used *ouija* boards, *Dungeons and Dragons,* and astrology. To sucker us in. To get us interested in his lies — particularly *any* alternative to Jesus Christ as the one hope for the world. In front of me, I see a newspaper headline from *Florida Today* newspaper.

Have you hugged your ALIEN today? proclaims the headline. The half-page features psychic Pat Raimondo, speaking locally at a "UFO Workshop." Aliens, she says, have beautiful truths for humanity. She downplays any devotion to little green men:

"'What I'm trying to do is share with people things that they're interested in.' Who better to tackle the subject, says Raimondo, than somebody like herself who is more attuned to other worlds?

"'Take a shaman (a priest-doctor or spiritual guide) for example,' she says, 'A shaman teaches you to penetrate other realms of reality. In those UFO encounters, the person is placed in an altered state of consciousness. Ultimately, it doesn't matter if it's a shaman or a UFO, the function is to educate the soul.'"

UFOs educating the soul? Wait a minute! Do you see anything sneaky going on here?

I do!

Read on:

"RAIMONDO'S EXPLANATION IS BACKED UP by observations [of UFO kidnap victims who returned] who say their experience has changed their world view.

"'What's the end result of this?' she asks. 'It causes people to think if there is a God, if they should seek out Truth. It definitely leaves a person changed. It starts to penetrate into their reality. It makes people ponder more.'

"…Three years ago, Raimondo was meditating when she received instructions to leave her psychic church in Melbourne [Florida] and establish another one in Texas …

"The church stresses that development of psychic 'gifts' that everyone possesses at birth. The church also includes elements of Christianity.

"Cheri Nichols, owner of the Starlight Aquarian Age store in Melbourne and an active member of the church, describes it this way:

"'We accept Jesus. We do read scripture. People are encouraged to manifest their gifts, developing peace and spreading light and love.'

"An editor of *The Lightworker,* billed as 'Brevard's New Age Network Paper," Nichols says the UFO topic was chosen partly because she has noticed a surge of interest from her clientele, who come each week to browse through a variety of meditation tapes, crystals, books and videos."

That's scary!

Noted author Dr. I.D.E. Thomas, a pastor in California has written an interesting book called *The Omega Conspiracy*, which was published by Growth Publishing. It was exerpted and condensed in a *DOVE Christian Magazine* article in August, 1987 called *Is There Something Demonic About Those UFOs?*

Here's what Dr. Thomas has to say about demons, Satan and flying saucers:

A THOUSAND YEARS BEFORE COLUMBUS, ancient Mayans and Toltecs of Central America knew and used penicillin.

Centuries before David Livingston penetrated the Congo jungles, the ancient Dogon civilization of the West African Republic of Mali knew of a satellite circling the star Sirius—a star in the constellation Canis Major, 8.5 light years away from Earth. Dogon wisemen also knew the satellite's position, gravitation and orbit. European astronomers did not find the star's white satellite until 1844, and it was not seen by telescope until 1862.

The Assyrians of 1440 b.c. drew pictures of the light in the sky that we call Saturn and circled it with a ring of serpents. How could they know of Saturn's rings? They depicted no other planet in this way. They also recorded the different phases of the moon with an accuracy not seen again until the 17th century a.d.

How did the ancient Greeks know that there were seven stars in Pleiades? They could only see six! Did a higher intelligence inform them?

Where did the Sumerians of Mesopotamia come from?

According to researchers Alan and Sally Lansburg, "They pop up like some devilish jack-in-the-box, around 3,000 B.C., fully equipped with the first written language, sophisticated mathematics, a knowledge of physics, chemistry and medicine."

THE PRE-INCA MOUNTAINEERS OF PERU performed amputations, bone transplants, cauterizations, brain surgeries and a variety of other complicated operations. From whom did they learn their advanced surgical skills?

Above the Bay of Pisco a giant pictograph in the rock, measuring 820 feet in size, forms a mammoth trident pointing heavenwards. The pictograph seemingly could not have been planned from the ground.

To view it, one has to fly above it. Yet when it was made 2,000 years ago, men supposedly had no means of flight.

Who engineered this mammoth undertaking?

And to what purpose?

SOME WOULD CREDIT TRAVELERS FROM SPACE. I think not, although legends tell of enormously wise, supernaturally powerful, heavenly beings—such as Apollo and Zeus—who visited among men, married, fathered half-human children and taught great secrets — then departed and were worshiped as gods.

The Aztecs of Mexico in particular traced their sciences back to a blond, blue-eyed being called Quetzalcoatl—whose symbol was a serpent. The Aztec Empire fell when his worshipers welcomed cruel Spanish explorer Cortez as their much-missed god.

Were these beings from outer space? *I say no. I believe the source is considerably more insidious—the result of an ancient deception straight from hell, setting the stage for a modern deception meant to draw men away from God as we near the final battle between good and evil, between God and Lucifer — between the Christ and the Antichrist.*

LOOK AT ONE OF THE OTHER FRUITS *of these encounters between men and these mysterious, legendary beings: cruel, hideous religions that included sexual perversion and ritual murder.*

Quetzalcoatl's cult required frequent human sacrifice.

I believe the growth of demonic activity in our time is proof of our proximity to the "last days" and to the mightiest power encounter of all history.

We may well be witnessing the opening scenes of the final act of a deception that has an ancient, evil purpose far beyond even the imagination of the creators of such space-visitor-focused Hollywood movies as:

- *Close Encounters of the Third Kind,*
- *E.T.: The Extraterrestrial,*
- *The Flight of the Navigator,*
- *Starman,*
- *Howard the Duck,*
- *The Last Starfighter,*
- *The Day The Earth Stood Still,*
- *The War of the Worlds and, of course,*
- *The three StarWars epics and all the resulting clones.*

"No matter where you live on this planet someone within 200 miles of your home has had a direct confrontation with a frightening apparition or inexplicable 'monster.'" So writes John Keel, one of the world's leading authorities on psychic phenomena and unidentified flying objects. "There is a chance—a very good one—that sometime in the next few years you will actually come face to face with a giant, hair-covered humanoid or a little man with bulging eyes, surrounded by a ghostly greenish glow."

A FEW YEARS AGO, UFOS WERE SCOFFED AT, *but in view of hundreds of witnesses, one is tempted to ask: Who are these beings? From where do they come? Whither do they go? What is their mission? Why do so many of the reports include detailed "truth" about the afterlife, God and* even Jesus. Some people who tell of contact with UFO occupants report that the beings quote from the Bible. Obviously, the fact that anyone quotes Scripture does not prove much. Satan also quotes the Bible — often for a seemingly benevolent purpose. When he suggested that Jesus turn stones into bread, what could have been more humanitarian?

And here is another troubling matter: Many of their messages contradict the Gospel of Jesus Christ. They advocate such propositions as:

* An impersonal God;
* Reincarnation and endless improvement in the hereafter;
* Men are not lost sinners in need of divine mercy;
* Christ was divine only in the sense that all men are divine; and
* Christ's resurrection was a mere materialization.

What is the purpose of these beings?

CONFUSION, I BELIEVE. ONE MORE FALSE HOPE. One more bogus alternative to repentance and redemption through Christ Jesus.

If they are from distant planets, how are they so well versed in the Christian religion? Why do they offer "revelations" about our God?

I belive the answer is plain. In fact, they have at times inadvertently betrayed their lineage. A notable number of contactees claim to have received messages from a "Mr. Ashtar."

Who is this personage? We seem to have met the name before. Ashtar or Ashtaroth, (Ashtoreth), was a Canaanite god.

ASHTAR WAS KNOWN IN BABYLON by the name of Ishtar, and in Ethiopia by Astar, whose worship was characterized by lewd and licentious behavior. It was one of those religions which perverted its adherents. The tree of life became a phallic image. Such were the obscene orgies and vile practices associated with the cult of Ashtar that it became an abomination unto the Lord.

Nowhere in the Old Testament does God's anger reach such a boiling-point as when He decreed the complete extermination of Palestine's pagan tribes. They had brought the land of Canaan to an all-time low in moral degradation. Such was its condition that Almighty God could no longer permit the situation to continue; their extermination had become a moral necessity.

The bottom line in all this is: Ashtar very well could have been **a real personage.** A fallen angel sent to confuse men and lead them astray. A demonic warrior masquerading as a god.

And I believe that such immortal, demonic beings are still here, active—and readying for the final battle. Remember that angels do sometimes appear in visible form.

THE BIBLE ADMONISHES, "BE NOT FORGETFUL *to entertain strangers, for thereby some have entertained angels unawares" (Hebrews 13:2).*

Abraham was visited by three men in the plains of Mamre (Genesis 18:1-8). They walked, talked, sat and ate, just like any other man. But actually they were not human at all, but spirit-beings from Heaven. Two of the three later visited Lot in Sodom and spent the night at his home.

If God's angels can take human form to communicate messages from the Lord, does it not stand to reason that demonic angels can take on similar form to practice their wiles — including to trick man into putting false hope into "galactic saviors from space?"

25

DEMONS? JUST PART OF THE PACKAGE!

Nicky, you may say,

with a sophisticated snicker on your lips, "Now, now, Nicky — you don't really believe in *demons*, do you?"

Listen, it doesn't matter what I believe.

The Bible describes them in great detail. Here's a list of Scriptures that you can look up for yourself if you want to see what the Bible says about whether they exist or not:

- Demons are spirits without bodies (Ephesians 6:12)
- They were originally angels (Jude 1:6)
- They possess humans (Mark 5: 8,9, Matthew 12:43-45, Luke 8:2)
- They have supernatural power (Revelation 16:14)
- They fear God (Matt. 8:29, Mark 1:23, James 2:19)
- They can cause illness (Matthew 9:32, 34, Mark 5:2-5)
- They teach false doctrines (I Timothy 4:1)
- They give Christians opposition (Ephesians 6:12, I Peter 5:8)
- God is going to have the last word (2 Peter 2:4).

But, you may ask, does demonic possession still happen today?

I've seen it. I know it does. But perhaps you would like to hear the testimony of a good, solid, fundamentalist, the very conservative Walter Martin, who has written extensively about cults and false teachers in the church.

Here's what he experienced, as told in his book *Exorcism: Fact or Fable:*

"Recently in the San Fernando Valley of California, three husky clergymen tried to hold down a 120-pound girl who was possessed with multiple demons. She successfully resisted all three of them for a number of minutes ... demonstrating tremendous supernatural power.

"In Newport Beach, California, I encountered a case of demonic possession in which five persons, including myself, were involved. In this case, the girl, who was about 5-feet-4 and weighed 120 pounds, attacked a 180-pound man and with one arm flipped him 5 or 6 feet away. It took four of us, including her husband, to hold her body to a bed while we prayed in the name of Jesus Christ for the exorcism of the demons within her.

"During the course of the exorcism, we found out that she was possessed because she had worshipped Satan, and because of that worship, he had come with his forces and taken control of her. She was a perfect 'tare in the wheat field,' as Jesus said in Matthew 13:24-30. She had married a Christian, was a daughter of a Christian minister, had taught Sunday school in a Christian church, and had appeared on the surface to be perfectly consistent with Christian theology. But the whole time, she was laughing inwardly at the church and at Christ. It was not until her exorcism that she was delivered and received Jesus Christ as her Lord and Savior. Today she and her husband are on the mission field, serving Jesus Christ.

"I have a psychologist friend who was present with me at an exorcism in Newport Beach, California. Before we entered the room, he said, 'I want you to know I do not believe in demonic possession. This girl is mentally disturbed.'

"I said, 'That may well be. We'll find out very soon.'

"As we went into the room and closed the door, the girl's supernatural strength was soon revealed. Suddenly from her body a totally foreign voice said quietly, with a smirk on the face (she was unconscious, the psychologist testified to that), 'We will outlast you.'

"The psychologist looked at me and said, 'What was that?'

"'That is what you don't believe in,' I said.

"We spent about three and a half hours exorcising what the psychologist didn't believe in!

"At the end of the exorcism, he was not only a devout believer in the personality of the devil, but in demonic possession and biblical exorcism as well. He now knows that there are other-dimensional beings capable of penetrating this dimension and of controlling human beings!"

Whenever I preach,

I'm conscious of two others on the platform beside me. *I know Jesus is there with me*.

He stands at my side, yearning for those who don't know Him to turn to Him and find His love. He gives me words to tell to each new audience what He has done in my life, and how much He can do for anyone else. When I finish speaking and men and women and young people start coming forward to take a new stand for God, I can sense His Spirit pleading with them, drawing them toward His loving arms.

But I know that Satan is there too. I know he has tried his best to keep various individuals from coming to the meeting. Whenever there's a disruption I can feel his attempts to create disorder and keep people from hearing what God wants them to know, to distract their thoughts, to prevent them from making a definite decision for Christ. I know that the struggle between Satan and Jesus is always taking place, and will never end until this age itself ends and God and Jesus are finally completely victorious.

YOU CAN SEE THAT STRUGGLE between the two invisible armies all through the Gospels.

• An angel appeared to Mary to announce that Jesus was going to be born (Luke 1:26-38).

• An angel appeared to Joseph to confirm His virgin birth (Matthew 1:18-24).

• Angels were glimpsed again and again during His birth and childhood, according to the first two chapters of both Matthew and Luke. When He grew up and was tempted, angels came to help Him (Matthew 4:11).

• When He struggled in Gethsemane in prayer, an angel came to bring Him strength (Luke 22:43).

• When He was arrested He said He could summon multitudes of angels to help Him if He so disired (Matthew 26:53).

• And angels rolled the stone away from His grave (Matthew 28:2).

ASK THE AVERAGE PERSON WHAT JESUS DID and he's likely to say, "He set a good example." He may add, "Jesus also taught about God." He may possibly also say, "He healed sick people."

What many people don't know is that Jesus also spent much of His time casting out evil spirits.

• The first opposition to Jesus mentioned by Mark was from a man possessed by an unclean spirit (1:23).

• Early in His ministry He cast out many demons (Mark 1:34; 3:11).

• And He continued this work of deliverance all through His life.

No wonder the prince of the demons, Satan, fought so hard against him!

• Satan tried at the very beginning to destroy Him, first by the sword of Herod (Matthew 2:16),

• Then by direct temptation (4:1-11).

After all, if he had persuaded Jesus to turn against His Father and sin, what a great victory it would have been for hell! But Jesus stood every test.

When I encounter scoffers,

people who want to ridicule the very idea of demons or Satan, I am amused at their lack of information. How else do you explain my father's psychic powers, my mother's occult gifts or the horrifying experience of Olga? How else can they be explained?

Delusions? *Fairy tales?*

There are plenty of theories about the occult. But the only explanation that really makes sense to anyone like myself who grew up in the middle of it, is the answer I found when I first got a Bible from Dave Wilkerson and started reading it.

I began at the first verse of Genesis. Everything I read was like turning on the lights in a dark, dirty dungeon.

First, all the bugs fled under rocks and into cracks.

Then, I began to see things as they really are.

I WAS AMAZED TO FIND HOW MUCH the Bible explained: the beginning of the world, the beginning of life, the beginning of human beings and the beginning of evil.

When you mention the devil many people think of a repulsive being, but they're only half right. What struck me hardest when I started reading Genesis was how attractive the serpent was.

A pretty snake? Read the Scriptures carefully and you'll see that Eve wasn't upset by the sight of a snake up in the tree at all. Read Genesis 3:14 -15 and you may be surprised to find that before that, apparently, snakes didn't have to crawl on their bellies and that women weren't scared of them. So, it would seem, Satan hid his ugly appearance by taking on the appearance of a lovely, sparkling snake.

I don't believe Eve would ever have fallen for Satan's lies if she could have seen him in his true, hideous nastiness. He knew better than to show his horrible face. So he entered into the body of a glittering serpent and spoke with all the appeal of a slick Madison Avenue pitchster.

Read the third chapter of Genesis and see for yourself. You'll find he is still using the same tricks to try to get hold of all of us! He knows how to fascinate, attract, possess.

When I first read Genesis 3, everything it said about Satan sprang out at me from the pages of the Bible. The devil has a strong influence — he's someone to keep away from! Glibly, smoothly, he contradicted what God had said. *And she believed him.*

HIS TEMPTATION OF ADAM AND EVE reminded me vividly of my own confrontations with him. At the same time, as a new Christian I realized I would have to steer clear of his influence and even anything that had the appearance of any connection with him.

People defending witchcraft will tell you it's "the old religion." They argue that it was here before Christianity as though that made it better. There is some truth in what they say, just as there is a little truth in every good lie. That's what makes people believe it. Evil spirits have been around for a long time, as the very first pages of the Bible show.

WHEN YOU BEGIN TO SEE SUCH THINGS, don't say I didn't warn you! The devil and evil spirits exist!

But there's no reason for Christians to live in fear. We are covered by Jesus' blood! It is a shield that protects us completely.

In the Book of Job, you remember, Satan went to the Lord to get permission to put Job through many trials so that he would curse and renounce God. The Lord said, in effect, "Job is in your hands to do with as you wish, but you cannot touch his soul" (Job 2:6). Now Job was in love with God and trusted Him completely. He went through many trials, but they were used to bring him closer to the Lord, so he could say at the end, "I have heard of thee by the hearing of the ear, but now mine eye seeth thee" (42:5).

Once Satan even tried to take over Jesus, but He never gave in one moment. The devil had no power over Jesus.

And he has no power over anyone who trusts completely in Almighty God and His Son, the Lord Jesus Christ!

Like you and me!

26

CAN A CHRISTIAN BE DEMON-POSSESSED?

When I was a little boy,

I was playing with some other little kids in a winding brook near our home in Las Peidras. After we had been playing for a couple of hours, a boy named Pablo grinned as he pointed at my right leg: "Hey, Nicky, what have you got on your leg?"

I looked down and there was what looked like a little black leaf near my ankle. But when I tried to brush it off I couldn't. It seemed to be growing out of my leg and it felt like leather. I yelled, "Eeeeeek!" and ran for home.

One look and Mama said, "Sit down, Nicky." She told me to hold still while she poured some salt on the black thing until it shriveled up and fell on the ground. "He is a bloodsucker," Mama said. "He did something to your leg so you will keep bleeding for a while, but you will be all right."

I THOUGHT I'D NEVER STOP BLEEDING where the leech had fastened itself to my leg, but after awhile the bleeding stopped and before long I forgot all about it.

How can you have an evil spirit inside you if you are filled with the Holy Spirit?

You can't. But it's a different matter for non-Christians. For them, it's something like having a leech fastened to you, sucking out your blood. You're thinking about other things when all of a sudden you feel something black and awful. You try to get rid of the horrible thing, but there's no way unless you know how to do it.

Before Jesus came into my life and the evil spirits went out, I used to have terrible feelings of depression. Sometimes I would sit for hours at a time thinking the most lonely, despairing thoughts.

Other times I'd be filled with hatred and violence.

ANYONE MAY BECOME DEMON-POSSESSED — almost. Anyone but a Christian. I do not believe it is possible for a person who trusts in Jesus Christ to be filled with an evil spirit, or dominated by one.

I know that some Christian friends will not agree with me about this. I have even heard people talk about casting out "Presbyterian demons," "Methodist demons," etc. (I have friends in every denomination, and I think that is going too far!)

I know how strong and dangerous demons are. But I do not believe any demon can enter a dedicated Christian, because I know the power of God.

Let me say again I know the power of Satan. He is evil personified — his whole nature is against everything God stands for. He is doing a lot in the world today that is obviously against Christ, and we should beware of all that. However, I think Christians often give the devil more credit than he deserves.

Many Christians have problems in special areas of their lives. Some smoke, realizing they shouldn't. Some are depressed more than they ought to be. Some have too many fears. Now, one of the common practices in some circles today is to label such hang-ups "demons of tobacco," "demon of depression," etc., and to cast them out in the name of Jesus.

I THINK THAT IS OFTEN A COP-OUT. I believe it lets us blame too much of our own failures and laziness on the devil.

I know how Satan would like to trip us up with such sins. I know his hatred for Christ and His people — I know he can oppress even Christians with his power and malice. He can use the things of the world to tempt us and take our victory from us. Often the devil has put obstacles in my way in an attempt to keep me from victorious living. And if we allow ourselves to be weakened by those attempts, the devil can move right in and work on us with even more effect.

But the Lord works in our lives as we yield to Him. The combination of our will with His power is what changes our lives into His image. As long as we are willing, He does the work. (See John 3:16 — 1:12 — Revelation 3:20.) When we fail, it's not a shortage of divine power but a failure of our own wills. James 1:14-16 explains it this way: "But every man is tempted, when he is drawn away of his own lust, and enticed. Then when lust hath conceived, it bringeth forth sin — and sin, when it is finished, bringeth forth death. Do not err, my beloved brethren."

SO LET'S STOP GIVING SATAN THE CREDIT for our sins and hang-ups when our will is the deciding factor! Why try to put everything on Satan's shoulders?

Aware as I am of the power and malevolence of Satan, I am even more aware of the power and love of Jesus Christ, of the Cross that gave us life, and of the dynamic Holy Spirit in our lives. Scripture after Scripture comes to my mind as I think about the wonderful power of God.

"For the law of the Spirit of life in Christ Jesus hath made me free from the law of sin and death" (Romans 8:2)! "If God be for us, who can be against us? He that spared not his own Son, but delivered him up for us all, how shall he not with him also freely give us all things?" (Romans 8:31, 32). "For I am persuaded, that neither death nor things present, nor things to come ... shall be able to separate us from the love of God, which is in Christ Jesus our Lord" (Romans 8:38, 39).

In Ephesians Paul prayed that his readers might have the eyes of their understanding opened to know "...what is the exceeding greatness of his power to us-ward who believe, according to the working of his mighty power, which he wrought in Christ, when he raised him from the dead..." (1:19,20). The same power of God that raised Jesus from the dead is available to every one of us today!

In the second chapter of Ephesians Paul reminds us that before we were Christians we lived "...according to the prince of the power of the air, that now worketh in the children of disobedience" (v.2). But God has raised us up to sit in heavenly places with Christ, to do good works — not bad (vs. 4-6, 10). Again he prays that we will "...be strengthened with might by his Spirit in the inner man — That Christ may dwell in our hearts by faith..." (3:16, 17) and that we might be "...filled with all the fulness of God" (3:19). Then he praises the God who is "...able to do exceeding abundantly above all that we ask or think, according to the power that worketh in us" (3:20).

Other passages that make this so clear are Philippians 3:10 — Colossians 1:19, 20: Hebrews 2:14-18 — 4:14-16 — 1 John 4:4 — and many, many more. The Word of God emphasizes time and time again the omnipotence of Christ. Why then should Christians be fearful that some demon or spirit is going to invade them when they are off guard? When we are living in the victory of Christ, His power fills us — He dwells within us in His fulness — and nothing can separate us from that power against our will (Romans 8:35-39)! We have received His Spirit of glorious liberty (Romans 8:21), and not the spirit of bondage to fear (Romans 8:15).

MY CHRISTIAN LIFE IS BASED ON THE LIBERTY and freedom from fear I have with my Saviour. I don't need to walk in fear of demons or spirits, as long as I find victory in Jesus. If I begin to doubt and allow fears or temptations to get the best of me, then naturally Satan can use that to his advantage. But God's Word is so full of promises of victory, and Christ is so willing and able to keep those promises, I do not see any need to worry unnecessarily about Satan sneaking up and getting control of me!

We need the confidence of Philippians 1:6: "Being confident of this very thing, that he which hath begun a good work in you will perform it until the day of Jesus Christ." We need to be able to say: "…I know whom I have believed, and am persuaded that he is able to keep that which I have committed unto him against that day" (2 Timothy 1:12).

Those who teach that any Christian may be possessed by demons appeal to the story of Ananias and Sapphira in Acts 5. This man and his wife certainly seem to have been included among the believers who sold what they had and gave the money to the church (4:32-37). It is true that Peter told Ananias that Satan had filled his heart (5:3). So it does look as though this is an example of a Christian who became demon-filled, or perhaps I should say Satan-filled.

But there is belief and belief. The devils (demons) themselves believe — and tremble (James 2:19). They believe there is a God and a Christ and a Holy Spirit — in fact they know it very well! — but they have nothing that could be compared to a Christian's trust and allegiance! Ananias couldn't blame his sin on Satan — Peter said that Ananias himself had conceived his wicked idea in his own heart (5:4) and this wasn't just suddenly giving in to a temptation, as a Christian may do sometimes. The record shows that Ananias and his wife had deliberately planned the whole thing, and had even conspired together to tell the same lie so that they would not be found out (4.7-9). Think of all the evil planning this pair did, and all the action it took to carry out their plans. They agreed together to sell their property, to say they got less than they did, to turn this smaller amount over to the church, and to testify falsely to the whole thing if they were questioned independently. This was no ordinary sin. This was a wilful, deliberate, carefully-plotted sin against the church and against the Holy Spirit (5:3). No wonder Peter said that Satan had filled Ananias's heart!

I CAN PICTURE PETER TREMBLING before a servant girl and denying he knew Jesus. But I can't imagine any sincere Christian planning and conspiring to carry out the deliberate deception and spiritual theft that Ananias and Sapphira engineered. So this incident doesn't convince me at all that anyone can at any moment be filled with demons.

My friend, my prayer for you is that you will be so filled with the Holy Spirit that there will be no room for any evil spirits.

Satan will attack you and oppress you if he can. He attacked Job. He oppresses me sometimes. He even tempted Jesus! But I can never believe that our Father in heaven, the Father who saves us and keeps us and fills us, will let the devil get the best of us.

My prayer is that we Christians will learn to walk in Christ's fulness, with our feet on the ground, ready to seek and accept forgiveness. We need to put our complete dependence on Christ. "But if we walk in the light, as he is in the light, we have fellowship one with another, and the blood of Jesus Christ his Son cleanseth us from all sin" (1 John 1:7).

Fighting back

is an important part of this book. Well, let me share with you another effective tool. A good friend of mine has grown to put enormous stock in a very traditional form of prayer.

Fasting. This may seem too old-fashioned for some, but he says there is no denying its incredible effectiveness. He goes on a fast when there has been no answer in the face of a deep need. He describes each fast as a unique and beautiful experience that is filled with pain, doubt, joy and a new love for Jesus — and a new understanding of God's ways.

One lesson, he says, that he learns over and over is that our urgency is seldom God's urgency. For example, he says the times that he has gotten himself into financial difficulty due to over-commitment, the Lord has been slow to bail him out. Even in the face of fervent prayer and fasting, the Lord seems to allow my friend to experience the anguish of his unwise actions, then gently, lovingly resolves the crisis — but only after true heart-felt repentence has been experienced in my friend's heart.

Such over-commitment is this young businessman's great weakness

— and the Lord is sternly, lovingly showing him to quit getting ahead of the Father's timing.

MY FRIEND SAYS THE FIRST DAY of his fast is usually the worst. His hunger is overpowering. But he uses each pang as a reminder to pray. The second day is usually tough, too, he said. But by the third or fourth, the hunger eases. His body has begun to live off of his stored up fats. And his prayer is so much easier. His mind is clear. And the results are amazing.

The Lord touches his spirit and gently shows him truths in shaping up his life, his relationships and his business practices. His priorities come into clearer focus. And, the crisis that prompted the fast is invariably solved in a magnificent way — although sometimes the Lord just shows my friend that he must wait patiently and in faith for the Father to take the action ... action which my friend entered the fast believing must be immediate.

How long should you fast? My friend says three weeks is the longest he ever went — and that enormous strongholds of the devil were torn down that time — in a dramatic way.

But one-day fasts are effective, too, he notes. "I just have to be careful not to accept second-best," he told me. "Usually on the first day, I get a partial answer that I could accept as good enough. I really believe that Satan backs off — to get me to go off my fast. He wants to deceive me that the crisis is past."

Effective prayer

is not something that comes to everybody overnight. Kids prayers are an exception. Jesus noted in Matthew 18:10 that children are especially precious to the Father: "Beware that you don't look down upon a single one of these little children. For I tell you that in heaven their angels have constant access to the Father."

Some people use this verse to explain why youngsters' petitions before the Lord seem to be so much more effective than adults'. Perhaps it is because kids are so innocent and trusting. Or, indeed, maybe it has to do with their angels having constant access to the Father.

Can you imagine such a privilege — to be allowed to bask in the presence of God? I envy Moses. If you remember, he went up on Mount Sinai to receive the Ten Commandments and the rest of the Law *directly from God*. Oh, the power of the presence of the Lord! When Moses returned, he had to wear a veil because his face glowed, blinding everyone.

SO, HOW, PLEASE TELL ME, did the Israelites fall into such serious sin so quickly? As they sought their freedom from Pharoah, God performed such awesome miracles! Then Moses came back with, his face shining like a neon light!

Yet, they turned to terrible sin! That so angered the Lord that He forced them to wander around in the desert for 40 years until everybody but two had died. Except for Joshua and Caleb, only the generation that had been born in the Wilderness was allowed into the Promised Land.

So, how can you or I get into God's presence? When two or three Christians are gathered together, Christ promises that He is in our midst. And in a beautiful time of praise and worship, haven't you felt the presence of the Holy Spirit moving among God's people?

But unlike the way my parents called spirits, we must never think we can summon the Lord or command Him to bless us with His presence. Instead, we are allowed to wait upon Him with joy, faith and patience.

We develop a personal relationship as we spend quality time with the Father. That's why regular, daily quiet time with the Lord is so important. You will look forward to your appointment as you get into the habit. What a joy when you have to have a romance with Him! A divine love affair between you and the mighty Maker of All Things. "Draw nigh to me and I will draw to you," is the promise given to the prayer warrior.

Fervent prayer is so important

as you become a warrior. Look at the results of David Wilkerson's four-hour daily prayer time back when he was failing so terribly with our gangs.

If you remember, Satan was doing a real number on Dave. Doubt, fear and anger were welling up in his heart. He began to wonder why he had come on his absurd mission to win big-city street kids to Jesus.

AND HE FAILED MISERABLY on his first encounters. We thought he was insane, then we began planning to kill him.

But Wilkerson prayed. And prayed. *And prayed.*

He didn't have any cute, quick formulas for driving Satan back. Just a fervent desire to obey God—*and intense faith that the Lord would resolve this impossible situation.*

I, too, have enjoyed the results of fervent prayer in impossible situations — such as praying for the seemingly unthinkable: *that my Mama and my Papa might come to Jesus.*

27

THE BATTLE FOR MAMA

I have already told you

that Mama became a Christian and now is in heaven. You are probably waiting for me to say that she once lived in fear and despair — but that as a new Christian she lived in perpetual peace and joy.

It wasn't quite like that. After I became a Christian, my brother Frank wrote to my parents about this unbelievable thing that had happened to me. Nominally our family was Catholic, although I only went to Mass once or twice when I was small. At a very early age I decided all this God stuff was a lot of nonsense and stopped going.

There had been Protestants in Las Piedras. But our family had less use for them than for the strict Catholics who objected to our form of spiritualism. Papa used to say the Pentecostals were crazy and the Evangelicals were dead. "I have more power than they have," he once chuckled.

SO MAMA STRUGGLED ALL BY HERSELF with the new ideas that came to her from Frank's letters about the changes in my lifestyle, attitudes — and my new drive to become a *preacher* instead of a street thug.

Mama had many painful questions about my changes — and my new beliefs. For years she had asked herself where she had failed with me. She had always tried to lead a good life, and now, it didn't make sense that the black sheep in the family — *me* — had changed his color and wanted to lead the world to truth and goodness.

So, her heart was torn and troubled — there was no peace for many years. Mama had many questions about Jesus. To her he had always been a good spirit, and there was no question that she had always believed in God, according to what she knew about Him. So had Papa. They had always done their best — despite the absence of Jesus in their lives. They had tried to raise their 18 children to be good and *do good*.

In general my parents succeeded remarkably well. My sister Carmen and my brothers studied hard, married fine partners, and are raising their children to be like themselves — stalwart, conscientious individuals. They love their children and to a high degree are living up to my parents' dreams for them. Three of my brothers are in the ministry — and two of them gave up good careers to follow God's call.

DURING THE SECOND YEAR OF BIBLE SCHOOL, I went back to Brooklyn to work on the streets with Dave. At a street rally, I suddenly came face-to-face with Frank — whom I had not seen in a long time.

"Mama has been searching for you," he said, holding out a letter from Puerto Rico. "She asked me to find you — and to get you to promise to read this. She's dying, Nicky, and she wants to see you."

I took the letter, but did not open it. *Mama wanted to see me?*

"Read it," urged my brother.

"I will," I answered softly.

"Nicky, you gotta promise me."

"I promise," I said — sincerely.

"Nicky," he said, looking me in the eye. "You better go see her."

I nodded. When I was alone, I opened the letter. "My son, I ask you to give me the privilege to see you," it read. "I know that I hurt you so much. But now I am going to die, and I want to see. I cannot die with so much guilt and sorrow in my heart. But if you refuse to come, I will understand."

I wept over that letter. "How am I going to go to Puerto Rick now?" I asked myself. "After all these years, how am I going to face my Mama?"

For so many years I had *hated* her. I'd *blamed* her. She had robbed me of my childhood. She'd kicked me out into the streets, forcing me to hide in the forest and haunt the back alleys of Humacao. So many times as a boy, then a teen and now as a man, I'd replayed in my mind the horrible words she had spat at me — denouncing me as the son of Satan. She hated me, she had said — I had the "mark of Lucifer on my heart."

As a Christian, I'd tried my best to forgive her. I had sincerely tried. I knew I could not let a root of bitterness fester in my heart! I could not expect the Lord to forgive me or listen to my prayers if I could not forgive!

I had to forgive her. But … so many times I had laid my deep, horrible hurts on the altar, asking Jesus to take away the haunting memories, the aching hunger of a little boy desperate for love but finding only disapproval. Oh, the anger I had nurtured in my young heart! For so many years, I had plotted her murder! I had taken out my vengeance on the world at large — taking on the entire city of New York, battling the most vicious street gangs in the world, defying any policeman to be foolish enough to challenge me!

But now, faced with the reality of returning home to my witchcraft-practicing parents, I was stricken.

How could I do it? Was I ready for the spiritual battle?

THE LORD PROVIDED A MAN to pay for me to fly home. But still, I feared new confrontation … the accusations … and the demonic warfare that I would surely face. I remembered the enormous power of the terrible spirits around my home — which filled my mother and drove her to such evil. I had no reason to believe that anything had changed. So, I prepared prayerfully — with my friends and professors and fellow students and members of local churches interceding.

I was heading into battle! And I was just yet an untrained recruit — daring to take on the mighty forces of darkness. My mother, the feared *bruja* of Las Piedras, who knew the future and spoke with the dead. My father, mighty *El Taumaturgo*, the Miracle Worker, *El Curandero,* the Healer.

I WILL NEVER FORGET MY RETURN TO LAS PIEDRAS. *So little had changed.* I had not seen these places of my childhood in so many years. From my taxi-cab, I glanced around, filled with memories. Over there, I had wrecked my bike and scraped my knee. Over here, I had beaten up the playground bully. It was a very emotional experience as I pulled up to our hilltop compound, particularly when my little brother, Rafi — looking all grown up although he was only 12 or so— ran up and took my luggage.

So little was different, I saw, as he, my father, and my brothers Chelo and José-Chemon walked with me into the house. Although Papa was very friendly, he was also distant. He was watching me, I could tell. He was studying my sincerity. And he was feeling out the level of my "power."

My brothers took me in to see Mama. She was very ill —down to 89 pounds. Although she was weak, she tried to hug me. Then she kissed me. It was a very tender moment. I began to weep. I had longed for this for so many years. The loving touch of my Mama. Her hand on mine. Her kiss.

We were both crying. *I was completely broken.* I asked her to be patient with me, that I had something that I had to talk to her about. "Mama,"

I said, "Jesus loves you." I gave her my Bible. She nodded. She had been reading Frank's letters.

Then, I carried her into her room and placed her carefully on her bed. I could tell she was very tired. Some things would have to wait.

I went into what had been my room. My clothes were still hanging in the closet. I trembled and touched shoes I had left behind at age 15 when I was exiled to New York City. Shirts. Short pants. And I began to feel the dark, demonic forces around me. Softly they began to whisper lies. *You cannot touch us here,* they seemed to hiss in the stillness. *Who do you think you are? The great Nicky Cruz? We know who you really are. We were at your birth. We watched you grow up in fear. This is our turf. We defeated you over and over before. Now, we shall show you who is truly in charge!*

And I realized why my Papa was so reserved. He knew that a great, spiritual battle was underway. Now, he was standing back to watch. He wanted to know who would win — his spirits or my Jesus!

I was again filled with fear — which I denounced. But still it would not go away. I went for a walk. But still, the evil forces mocked me. *You will fail here,* rustled the trees. *You are no match for us,* laughed the brook.

TREMBLING, I RETURNED TO THE HOUSE. I changed clothes and ran out of the house. I needed help. I had to pray with fellow Christians. The Lord reminded me of a little church nearby. Yes! Maybe the pastor would hear my story.

As night fell, I ran toward the building, I was so thrilled to hear singing. I was even more delighted to find that they were having a service. I sat down and enjoyed the sermon. Then pastor asked if anybody had a testimony they wanted to share. *I raised my hand.*

"I am Nicky Cruz, my father is Galo Cruz, the Great One, the *espiritista* healer. You all know him. I want all of you to come to my house and pray with me. I need help. I am a new Christian, and I don't know what to do for my family. Will you go with me to pray for them?"

A lady jumped to her feet — angry. "No," she spat, "we are not going to that place! That man is demon-possessed. That woman — your mother — is demon-possessed. Your brothers are demon-possessed and even your dog ..." Rafi had a pup named Tuti. "... that dog is demon-possessed!"

But the pastor understood. "Yes! Of course!" he declared, "We are going. We *will* help you, Nicky. We will go to the Spirit House to pray for your family with you."

The next morning, I knew there was something I had to do. I went into town and bought Mama a very beautiful dress and some nice perfume. When I came back that afternoon, I helped her wash her face. I combed her greying hair and helped her put on the dress. Then, as night fell, I picked her up and carried her onto the living room sofa.

I was overcome with emotion. I realized that I could do nothing for her. Only God could touch her — *change her* — and save her soul.

AT SUNSET, THE CHURCH PEOPLE CAME, just as they promised. And they came ready for battle — I could hear them singing and rejoicing as they walked up the hill. Those precious Christians brought guitars and tambourines and accordions. And, oh, how they sang and praised the name of Jesus! They were such noisy folks. I was so happy to have them up there!

Little did I know that God was about to soak our hilltop with his presence — and give us all of us a tiny preview of how Christian brothers and sisters will love one another when we get to heaven.

More than 500 had gathered from all over — good local Christians, who had sworn that they would never come up to our evil house of witchcraft. They sang and worshiped Almighty God and proclaimed the salvation of the Lord through Jesus Christ.

As if he were frightened by such power, my father disappeared into the shadows of the forest — where he watched us unseen. Oh, the spectacle that our Lord God prepared for Papa. All around him, the mighty light of God drove back the frightened, powerless forces of darkness!

Inside the house, the pastor and many believers crowded into the living room. He asked me to say a few words. I was so moved that I just began to cry. I could not say a thing. Then, I felt tender hands on my face and I looked up and could not believe it — it was Mama!

She was crying, too — washing the windows of heaven with her tears. She kissed my hands as I knelt beside the sofa. Then, she whispered something to me. "My son," she said. "I want to give my life to this Jesus who has changed you so much."

I just fell to my knees and grabbed my mother by the head and kissed her, and kissed her, and kissed her. And I completely forgave her — *absolutely* this time. And in the heavenlies, our Father did, too.

The angels rejoiced! And the battle was won! The demonic forces hadn't been given even a chance! *Oh, the joy that filled my soul!*

Because I had obeyed, you know what God did? He gave a hurting little boy his beloved Mama! My dear, wonderful mother! Not the wicked, ugly woman possessed by demons and spitting hatred at me — but my marvelous Mama, the loving woman who had given me life, bounced me on her knee, and whom I had longed for in the dark nights.

SHE WAS SAVED THAT EVENING. She was ripped apart with terrible conviction of her sin, fell on her face in repentence — and was forgiven!

"Oh, Jesus," she cried aloud. "I have been so wrong for so many years! But I did not mean to hurt you! Forgive me, Lord! Forgive me!"

That night, she was joyously filled with God's Holy Spirit and completely healed. She actually got up off of the sofa, praising God — a completely new person! She was healed of diabetes, heart problems, circulation difficulties — and given the strength to live another 25 years!

Oh, the joy! For decades, I had hungered for the love of a mother who cared about me. And now, God gave me the deep desire of my heart!

And, yes, everything changed when Mama came to Jesus. It was the beginning of some wonderful things. Before long, three of my brothers were in Bible institutes. Frank became a missionary in Central and South America, and is today a pastor in Puerto Rico.

For Mama it was the beginning of such a new kind of life. She was filled with a peace and joy that he had never seen before. Instead of communing with evil spirits, she began praying for two hours a day — not because anyone told her she had to, but because she wanted to fellowship with her new-found Shepherd as much as possible.

There were so many things to talk over with Him.

BECAUSE PAPA LOVED MAMA SO GREATLY, he did not oppose her in any way. But he remained skeptical. He could not deny the supernatural spectacular he'd watched — nor the enormous defeat of his spirit allies.

In deep respect for Mama and her new beliefs, he gave her enormous latitude as in the next years she grew in local reputation as a holy woman — a kind, beautiful Christian saint. One night great flames lit the sky on our hilltop in Las Piedras. Neighbors rushing up from the village to help my family fight the fire were startled to see Mama standing in our driveway with her arms folded while the two Spirit Houses crackled in flame.

"I set fire to them myself," Mama declared. "There will be no more spirit seances. We will worship only one spirit now — God's Holy Spirit."

But believing isn't simple

nor effortless for anyone. Those genuinely committed to Christ face a constant struggle — and for those once involved in the occult, the struggle is multiplied many times. The spirits that Mama renounced would not give her up. They were always after her. Many of Mama's former spiritualist friends, of course, were bitterly opposed to her Christian stand. They saw it as an attack on what they were doing.

And of course it is—praise Jesus! So they attacked back — and my mother faced new hostility that she did not anticipate. In her Las Piedras church Mama found fellowship and strength. But there was deep division and bitterness there too. Surely Satan is hard at work, even within believers.

Satan always attacks, of course, at our weakest points.

Before, with my father at her side, Mama never had to be afraid. But, now, old and alone in her last years, she was subjected to frightening incidents. Just two weeks before I visited Mama in the summer of 1972, one of my brothers came to her house at 1:30 A.M. and knocked in the special way he has to let her know who it was. She opened the door and let him stay for the night, as he sometimes does.

At 4:30 A.M. Mama was awakened by exactly the same steps on the porch, exactly the same pattern of knocking as before. She went to the door and no one was there.

THINGS LIKE THIS often happened to my mother once she became a Christian. She was more afraid than the average woman would be, for she knew the malevolent power behind the strange noises and inexplicable events that came to her. But she also knew the Savior who guarded her with His own mighty power.

"Once I lived in peace," Mama said to me before her death, "because the devil was sure I was his. Now that I have come out of the darkness into the light, he is like an angry lion. His demons are always around me, but so are Christ's angels, and Christ is stronger than all the demons."

Yes, frightening things happened to my mother after she met Christ, but much more worse ones happened to Papa.

28

ONE PRIZE THE DEVIL DIDN'T WIN

When they were in witchcraft

my father and mother did not like to admit they were being used by evil spirits. They said many times they were helping people through the aid of "good spirits."

But they knew the truth. Papa was so deeply under spirit domination — *slavery* — that he spent nearly 80 years without Christ.

My father told me of the torture that began when he first seriously considered joining Mama and me in a clear-cut decision to enthrone Jesus Christ as Lord and Saviour.

"It has been torture, Nicky," he said from his white hospital bed. "The spirits came to me from the north and the south, the east and the west. They told me they would take away all my power and protection. They said they would kill me the instant I publicly came out for Christ. They threatened to torture and kill every member of my family.

"I KNOW THEIR POWER, NICKY," he sobbed. "I have given my life to what I thought was a good thing. Now I see clearly they were lying and deceiving."

"There is no power like God's, Papa," I said.

"I know it, Nicky. You have proven it in your life. But spirit power — that is real too, Nicky. I want to be a Christian, my son, but I don't dare."

I wished I could stay in Las Piedras and give Satan the biggest fight of all eternity! How I would have liked to battle him for my father's soul!

But I am not the Archangel Michael and God was calling me to other work. I do not underestimate the power and cunning of man's oldest adversary. I would not have dared to touch my father without a clear indication from above. I cannot think of anything more dangerous than dealing with evil spirits. There are cases that yield to nothing but prayer and fasting and at that time I did not have the time nor the command to win my father's soul from the enemy. That work was to be done by others.

ABOUT FOUR YEARS BEFORE HE DIED, Papa was taken with a malady the doctors did not understand. As he went in and out of the hospital, Papa drew great strength from a man named Choco Davila.

Choco was a thoroughly Christian businessman. Weekdays he ran his business, supplying materials for various construction projects. Saturdays, Sundays, evenings, and as often as possible on the job, Choco Davila worked for the Lord. He was an outstanding member of his church. When it was testimony time, he was rarely without an expression of thankfulness for what God had done for him. When the pastor was away, Choco often filled the pulpit. And what sermons he preached! While my father had little use for most sermons and preachers, he loved the messages Choco gave. So he often went to hear Choco speak.

CHOCO WAS A FAR CRY from the hellfire-and-damnation preachers who sometimes fill our Puerto Rican pulpits. Papa liked him because what he said was always intelligent and never condemnatory. Yet he preached the message of the Bible. From Choco's sermons it was clear that spiritualism is definitely not a way to heaven, but Choco never denounced spiritualism — although he hated it passionately. He just explained what the Bible said, so clearly and attractively that it was hard not to agree.

Choco Davila visited our home many times during Papa's last years. On one of his first visits, he read the Bible and talked — and Papa wept. Then Choco put his hands on Papa's head and began to pray.

PAPA WAS SITTING IN A ROCKING CHAIR in our living room. Underneath the rocker slept his dog, Diablo. As Choco laid his hands on Papa's head, Diablo leapt up with a growl like a lion roaring and charged with such fury that Choco ran from the house. Choco promised to come back, and did, but Papa said: "When anything good comes into my life, something like this always happens."

Mama read the Bible to Papa during those last years. On one occasion, as she read, both she and Papa saw tongues of fire leaping up from the pages. Papa had never read the second chapter of Acts, I'm sure, nor ever talked about tongues of fire. But he knew a miraculous sign when he saw one. From that moment he was convinced what he must do.

The last time Papa was in the hospital, many mediums came to visit him and many other people tried to get in to seek his help as they had done in the past. There were also many Christians who came to witness to him.

I HAD A WONDERFUL TALK WITH PAPA in the hospital. He said: "My son, I want Christ. The spirits keep coming to me, threatening me with what they will do to me and to all of you if I ask Christ to come in. I am still afraid of them, Nicky. But my choice is made. I am going to give my life to Jesus, Nicky. When I do this, I will ask Him to take me then."

Soon after, Papa returned to our home. I had to return to the United States. Papa asked Mama to invite Choco to come in again, and he spoke simply but eloquently of Jesus and His love. He read to Papa from the third chapter of John and the eighth chapter of Romans. When he prayed for Papa, Papa gripped Choco's hand. Then he called Mama.

"Aleja," said my father to my mother with a tremendous light in his face. "I have done it! Jesus is mine! Gloria a Dios! Alleluia!"

Eight hours later Papa died.

Jesus took him home as he had asked and the devil lost a prize at the very gates of death.

More than 500 people came to my father's funeral in Las Piedras. It was the biggest funeral the village ever had. My sister and brothers and I cried like babies when he was buried, and we were not the only ones.

I have often thought what a tremendous Christian my father would have made if he had come to Jesus earlier. He had such tremendous gifts and insight — he could spot a phony a mile off, and he gave of himself the best way he knew.

Well, now he has all eternity to serve his Savior. May his life speak, too, through this memory of a man who was truly great.

29

DEVIL ON THE RUN!

As my flight took off,

taking me to a speaking engagement in South Bend, Indiana, I struck up a conversation with the woman in the next seat. When I told her about this book, which I'd just begun writing, she bristled like an angry cat. "I can't believe in demons and devils," she said. "And even if you were right, would a good God torment such beings in hell? I wouldn't be that mean myself."

"Lady," I said, "I don't just believe in demons, I *know* they are real. And I wouldn't call it mean to leave them to the evil they love. But it's not up to you or me to judge God. He is the Judge. One thing I'm sure of: There is no condemnation for those who are in Christ Jesus!"

The woman turned away, pushed her call button and ordered a double martini. She didn't speak to me again.

I WONDERED IF I SHOULD I TRY TO TELL HER about the demons on my recent trip to the South American country of Paraguay. Over 2,000 witches had been preaching and praying against us as we began a crusade in the capital of Asuncion. Yet, the Christians of Paraguay were praying, too — with great faith for a national revival.

During the crusade — on one night in particular — 45,000 people gathered in the national stadium. The movie, *The Cross and the Switchblade* had been on national TV three times, so, we had a lot of interest. But that night, it was as if there was a cloud of evil hanging over the place.

I could feel the power of Satan trying to choke us. I turned to one of my Paraguayan brothers. "We must pray," I whispered to him. "That crowd is Lucifer — *the power of death."* People on the stage and behind it began to seek the Lord's help. And the evil broke. In the presence of the faith of God's people, Satan must retreat. The cloud parted.

The Lord allowed me to speak with power and authority. About 45 minutes into the service, I opened the altar and more than 5,000 people began streaming down the aisles, coming to the Lord. Satan didn't like that. He launched a counterattack. We suddenly had more than 250 satanists running all over — screaming, cursing, generally trying to take over.

So, I again took authority in the name of Jesus. We prayed for them. Dramatically, in the midst of that vast crowd, they were delivered. They fell, screaming and shaking as their demons fled. Officials of the Paraguayan national Red Cross wanted to take them to the hospital.

I told the medics "Don't touch them." *They are OK.* Jesus has freed them. They don't need man's medical treatment."

I glanced at the woman in the airplane seat next to me. How could I get her to understand such an experience — or my need to write a book helping Christians to know how to fight back?

IN SOUTH BEND I WAS GREETED BY FRIENDS who had booked me into a county fair. Then Edward Grayling and his wife invited me to rest in their home during the two hours that remained before the meeting. But I couldn't rest. I had to be by myself. Grateful for the woods that stretched up a long sloping hill behind the Graylings' home, I plunged into the trees, exulting in the fresh air and the singing of lots of birds.

Sometimes before I preach I feel like I'm standing on a snow-covered mountain with the snow beginning to melt and rush down into streams. I sense the potential of God to use my words to bring parched souls the water of life. But this time, "O God," I said, "I am so tired. In two hours I am going to be standing on that platform in front of thousands of people. I don't know who will be there, but I want to do my best for You. It's such a miracle to see different ones coming forward to You, Lord. Yet I feel so dry. I've given my testimony so many times, sometimes it seems almost mechanical. Forgive me, Lord — don't let me ever be like a machine. Please help me to feel once more tonight the wonder of what You have done in my life as I tell my story. Let it come out fresh and meaningful. Give me Your power. And please, Lord, show me that You're there tonight."

I FELT BROKEN BEFORE GOD. Two or three mosquitoes bit me but I hardly felt them. I poured out my fears and mistakes and hang-ups. I asked Jesus to correct the things in my life that were not pleasing to Him.

Peace and joy began filling my heart. I felt the Lord's assurance that nothing done in His name is useless. The sadness that had been dogging me since my chat with the woman on the plane began disappearing in the warmth of a wonderful sense of the loving presence of my Father in heaven.

I knew that the devil was on the run!

The Lord reminded me of my recent trip to Holland, where five high priests challenged me to debate. Instead, the power of the Lord swept through our meeting hall and two of the Satanist leaders fell to their knees in awe of Almighty God and gave their lives to Jesus!

And as I drank in the wonderful country atmosphere, an answer came to me for the question that woman on the plane had asked me: "Would a good God torment such beings in hell?"

God doesn't torment, I realized. He lets us choose life or death, blessing or cursing. God makes the air and the sunshine. It is man and Satan that pollute and destroy. I remembered a party I went to when I was with the gangs in Brooklyn. The air inside the crowded room was so thick with the stench of pot and tobacco and rum and cocaine, walking into it was like stepping into hell. None of us had to be at that party. We had created that filthy air ourselves — we had freely chosen to breathe it.

And Satan, created for a position of great authority in heaven, chose hell. If he and his angels prefer eternal death to everlasting life, God is not going to stand in their way. God gives all of us the freedom to choose whether we want to spend time and eternity with Him or without Him. Satan and his followers have already made their choice.

WHILE THE COOL BREEZES RUSTLED through the leaves of the trees all around me there in Michigan woods, I thought of the wonders of God. Satan has his signs and marvels, but God performs genuine, lasting miracles. I thought of Sonny Arguinzoni, who is such a great servant of the Lord — and he had been down so low in sin! God has raised him up to have an outstanding ministry to 2,000 drug addicts in Los Angeles. He has a church with over 3,000 people! I love to call him my spiritual son.

I talked to the Lord there in the woods for a long time. Suddenly I noticed the sky was turning gray. Lightning flashed and there was a distant boom of thunder like the sound of a street rumble. It looked as though there was going to be a bad storm. I hurried back to the house and rode with the Graylings to the fair grounds. Three thousand people had been expected for the meeting, but the grounds were packed. A police lieutenant said, "There are about 7,000 people here."

They filled the big open-air amphitheater and stood in the aisles.

Soon after the service began, rain began to fall. I thought to myself that there was no way we would make it through the service. Raw gusts of wind roared through the bleachers, and the rain came in torrents. Lightning flashed, thunder boomed, and I felt that we were getting a preview of World War III.

THE PEOPLE WERE GETTING SOAKED THROUGH. I looked at that patient multitude and thanked God. I knew there were some beautiful Christians in the audience with great faith. I asked the Lord to take control. Then I asked the people to join with me in prayer.

"Lord," I said, "there are people here tonight who love You. There are people here who need Your help. There are many powers up there in the heavens, Lord, but You control them! All power is in Your hands. You have the power to stop this storm. We ask You for such a miracle. Amen."

Almost as soon as I said "Amen" the rain stopped. Amazement and delight spread over the faces in front of me. The crowd understood God answers prayer! The way was prepared for many to accept their Savior. And my own faith was stirred. I said in my heart, "Thank You, Father."

Then, as I told the story of Jesus and His love, I saw radiant smiles breaking out on faces glistening with rain. There were women in front of me with their hair plastered down all over their heads in dripping locks. Men in expensive suits looked like skid row bums who had slept in puddles. But God was among us — I felt His presence and concern for everyone there.

WHEN I ASKED THOSE WHO WANTED to follow Christ to come forward, I was amazed at the number who responded. Their shoes squished with water as they came down the aisles, their clothes dripped, but there was a spirit of expectancy and faith I have seldom seen.

As the service ended and counselors knelt inside with new converts, a flash of lightning split the sky. Thunder boomed in a deafening blast. Rain fell in torrents while people raced for their carsr. An announcement came over the loudspeakers that a tornado was coming in our direction. Once more nature went about its business. But in between the downpours, thousands of people had seen that God was on His throne.

How good He is to me!

I am covered by His protecting blood, and the devil can never touch my soul. And I am *so blessed* to be a spokesman for the King of Kings. He rewards me in such incredible ways. For example, just a few weeks ago, I had just returned from a crusade in Puerto Rico when my phone rang.

"Nicky!" greeted the voice. "This is Hector." *Hector?* My old buddy, Hector from the Mau Maus, *the guy with the sawed-off shotgun who had wanted to blow Wilkerson away?* I had been told that he was *dead!* "Nicky," he exclaimed, "Jesus is my Lord!"

My eyes filled with tears as he told me a nightmarish story. He'd gone down to the altar that when I gave my life to Jesus. But temptations had been too much. The next day, he'd gone out and robbed a laundry and beat up the owner. He'd been arrested, convicted — and spent five years in prison. In the penitentiary, he had gotten heavily into the occult and illegal drugs. As soon as he was paroled, he started dealing narcotics — and getting deeper and deeper into *espiritista* activities. Finally arrested for dealing, he went away for another ten years.

HE WAS RELEASED AGAIN just as I was holding my crusade in Puerto Rico. He had turned on a TV and watched an interview on secular television where I shared my testimony.

He was stunned. He didn't know I was still alive, either!

My story touched his heart. That Sunday, he went to a nearby church and gave his life to Jesus. Now, he was telling me on the phone, he was ready to launch into a ministry of evangelism.

"Praise God," I told him, knowing I had to fly to Puerto Rico immediately to talk with him. He might be feeling a great calling, but I needed to share with him lessons I had learned the hard way — such as learning to walk with the Lord ... instead of running ahead of Him.

I praise God for what He is doing today with Hector. I want you to know that I cried like a baby as I talked with him on the phone. Hector, too, broke down. "Hey, Nicky," he said, "once we were blood brothers in the Mau Maus. But now, I'm really your brother — for all eternity!"

I could only weep. *How wonderful is our God!* How incredible are our Lord's mighty ways!

And how Satan hates

it when he loses his children — like my Mama, my Papa, and Hector! His evil lies are so terrible! People get into the occult because they believe he will give them security, or will show them the future. Well, I prefer true security! And I know everything in the future that's important — mainly that God is in control and will show me anything that He thinks I need to know!

Satan offers bogus hope that results in dark, desperate disappointment. But God offers complete freedom and life! Through Jesus, He offers us eternal protection and blessing. Satan only has lying wonders. He fabricates mighty delusions. He is headed to eternal punishment with all his angels of darkness. What a horror that he has already been successful in taking billions upon billions of unsaved souls with him into the pit!

Did you know that there are more than 27,000 witches in America praying continually for demons to penetrate every Gospel-preaching church?

That's right. Paraguay isn't the only foothold of Satanism. It is increasingly strong on America's West Coast — and even in the "Bible Belt" of the Midwest. Specifically, I am told, American Satan worshipers are praying and fasting that ministers will fall, families be divided, and Christians will be a disgrace to their communities and to Jesus.

THAT'S THE REAL ENEMY AT WORK. What was Jesus trying to say when he kept praying, "that they all may be one?"

He meant that he desired all his followers to be unified in heart and purpose! I am bewildered when I look at the church. So many church groups fight with each other because of differences in *theology*. And while their battle rages, the lost and wounded sit huddled in emptiness and death.

Satan quietly beckons them to come with him and leave these bickering Christians behind. He has such new, exciting answers: Zen! Astrology! Meditation! The New Age Movement!

What a dispicable tragedy! What a lie!

I HAVE HEARD SATAN'S PRETTY LIES. I know he is real. I have fought him and — by God's wondrous intervention — won. One night in a Puerto Rico, I encountered Satan in a terrible way. Around midnight, I was jolted awake by a painful kick in the ribs. It threw me to the floor. I leaped up, at first believing someone was in the room, robbing or attacking me!

Then the room filled with a disgusting odor — a nasty stench that I recognized from my father's seances. And I knew no mortal had kicked me.

This was no nightmare. I had been thrown physically to the floor. I was in pain. I was shaken to my very foundations. I ran around the room, checking to make sure that nobody was there.

And suddenly, I remembered somthing Papa had shared with me: evil spirits love to attack the mind — blending fear and shame and confusion to trick victims into believing they are mad. Lucifer's putrid, mocking presence was all around me. I was truly terrified. "O Lord, help me!" I prayed, "I don't know what happened here. But, Lord, protect my mind!"

The room was silent. I knelt, trembling. "Protect me, Father. Surround me with your angels! Protect me with your mighty warriors! Don't let the devil trouble me!" And I felt strength and reassurance filling me. "Satan!" I called out. "In the name of Jesus, leave me alone!"

Then, the Lord did a mighty thing. He put me back to sleep. As I slept, I had a great peace all around me — which is hard to explain since I also sensed a mighty spiritual battle raging on my behalf.

I will tell you that I have no doubt that a great contest took place that night for purposes that I cannot begin to try and explain. God, in His mercy, allowed me to snooze through it. *This battle was His.*

When I awoke, I was completely refreshed.

I was renewed and unscathed.

THE NEXT DAY, AS I BOARDED AN AIRPLANE to my next crusade, I was confronted, face-to-face with an angry-looking woman — "How did you like that warning I gave you last night?" she demanded.

I stared at her, astonished. *What?* How did she know? Almost by instinct, "Get thee behind me, Satan," I ordered her, "in the name of Jesus!"

Her face paled as if I had punched her. She backed away, glancing around the airport corridor. Although there were people all around us, it was as if we were invisible. Nobody seemed to notice the scene.

She snarled her hatred as she retreated.

Realizing what was going on, "In the name of Jesus, GO!" I called in a spontaneous flood of bits and pieces of Scriptures. "I rebuke you! Jesus is eternal life and He is my Lord and King. Ours is not a spirit of fear, but of a sound mind! I will not fear, for the Lord is with me!"

She spat her defiance and backed away. *Then she was gone.* The people around us didn't even look up. Perhaps I should have been shaken. Maybe I should have canceled all my crusades and curled up at home, trembling in my boots that the mean, nasty devil was so naughty and daring.

Ha!

In my own strength, I would probably have done just that.

But I have a mighty Protector who does not allow me to even know the horrible plots that Satan and his angry hosts are trying to conjure up to hurt me and other Christians.

For some reason that night, the Lord had allowed Satan to reach me only for a moment. Then my God had blessed me with a deep sleep while He and His wonderful angels took care of the problem. *What a mighty God we serve!* He cannot lose.

For He alone is Lord of All!

I HATE SATAN AND ALL HIS DECEPTIONS. I hate what he tried to do to Miguel. I hate what he did to Olga. I resent the bondage in which he holds the people of Guatemala, Thailand and Zimbabwe.

And I hate what he did to my family. For centuries my forefathers lived under his horrendous curses. My father and mother practiced dark arts that they learned at their parents' knee. I grew up with people coming to them to be healed and to talk to the dead.

And I've even been kicked in the ribs by him!

I know what a terrible, real entity Satan is.

He is my blood enemy.

And he hates me. But through the blood of Jesus, I broke his grip on my family. *I found the cure for the curse.*

I learned that he has no power over me.

And, I pray, so have you.

If you would like to contact Nicky, please feel free to write to him at: **Nicky Cruz,** P.O. Box 25070, Colorado Springs, CO 80936

ADDITIONAL READING:
Destined to Win and "Brothers & Sisters, We Have a Problem"

If this book as helped you, we recommend that you find in your local Christian bookstore Nicky's exceptional book on personal holiness, which is available in Great Britain under the title Destined to Win.

In the United States, Australia, New Zealand, Singapore, Malaysia, the Republic of South Africa, Canada, Hong Kong, Ghana, Nigeria and other countries, the book is available under the title Destined to Win and also "Brothers & Sisters, We Have a Problem."

In the Spanish edition, the book is ¡Despiertase, Iglesia!

Nicly also has a new 90-minute video that shares his testimony, Nicky Cruz LIVE! For more information, feel free to write to DOVE Christian Books, P.O. Box 36-0122, Melbourne, FL 32935.